Hearing Jesus' Call
A Quantum Leap

Jean Khoury

Table of Contents

Introduction

All the chapters of this book, except one, have been taken from articles published on the School of Mary's website (www.schoolofmary.org). I believed it would be beneficial to make them available in a physical copy to reach a wider audience.

These articles typically address specific needs in teaching or provide answers to student inquiries. Their style often resembles spoken language, leading to imperfections and repetitions.

I faced the choice of either waiting several more years to perfect their style before publishing them or deciding to make them available as they are. I hope readers will understand and forgive any editorial flaws.

I dedicate this book to Our Lady, recognizing her vital role in our second conversion. Our Christian life can be divided into two periods: one before hearing Jesus' call and one after. This book explores certain aspects of Jesus' call that might be overlooked. However, it does not claim to be exhaustive. I am well aware that the second conversion deserves a thorough treatment, perhaps in the form of a course. I hope to undertake this soon, taking the example of St. Teresa of Avila.

Given the interconnected nature of spiritual topics, I often chose to refrain from adding more chapters to prevent the book from becoming overly challenging to read. Hopefully, readers will find additional information in past and future books or explore the School of Mary's website.

Jean Khoury

17th January 2024, St. Anthony the Great

A Call is a Call

We have been reminded by Council Vatican II of Jesus' call to every Christian for holiness. Everybody is called to become a saint (see chapter 5 in Lumen Gentium and the Catechism n°2013[1]). Although we are all called, there is a fine line between acknowledging the existence of that call, and taking for granted that we are all "naturally"/automatically called by God to holiness. There is a fine line between saying: "you are baptised, therefore you are called to holiness" and saying: "one day you'll hear in a clearer way Jesus knocking at the door of your heart, wanting to speak to you, showing you his love and calling you to follow him more closely". The difference between both cases is huge.

God is God

One takes for granted that it is almost like a "right" to be called to holiness, a right obtained in Baptism, and that therefore it becomes a "duty" for all Christians to work on it (we say: "to tend to it"). But in fact on one hand God is God, he is a real being, and not a machine that produces saints, he has his own views, his own "feelings", plans, wisdom, timing, initiative and on the other hand, we are not always ready to hear God's call.

The Infinite Enters into the Finite

A call in this case is the entrance of God, of Jesus, in our time, in our space, aiming at me, and only at me, as if I meant the entire world to him, and he wants to talk to me, to engage with me. A call is personal. You don't call a crowd to holiness, you call persons, individually, in a unique non-repeatable way.

He has the Initiative

Furthermore, God has the initiative, not us. Nobody can go to God through his own will, initiative, desire. God calls us. We want him? Well he wants us a million more times… let us try to hear his subtle voice in our heart.

---

[1] See the chapter before last, p. 143.

"Wisdom shouts loudly in the streets" (Proverbs 1:20) say the Holy Scriptures. Jesus is the Wisdom of the Father. Do you hear him shouting loudly in the streets?

Everything starts with this sight of love that Jesus gives to each one of us, in a unique way. "And Jesus looking upon him loved him, and said to him, 'You lack one thing [...], follow me'." (Mark 10:21) Nobody can replace Jesus' look. No doctrine, no morality, no rites or liturgies can replace that absolute initiative. It is indeed totally and radically his initiative.

We can facilitate that connection between Jesus and each human being, we can help people hear that subtle voice, in their heart, we can tell them that it is the case so they can become more attentive to him. We can teach ways to hear Jesus' voice. But nobody can replace Jesus' presence and Jesus' initiative. No plan on earth can do that. If the person that hears you telling them that Jesus has the initiative and they don't turn inwardly, into their heart, and they don't discern that subtle gentle breeze of Jesus' Call, well then all our projects are just human initiatives. Christianity is Christianity! It is not a man-made religion, or a man-made worship.

Can we Plan God's Call?

We can and have to facilitate Jesus' Call, of course, this is our duty as the witnesses of His Love, of the encounter with him. But "witnessing" is not "us calling". Here is what John the Baptist says about that point: "No one can receive anything except what is given him from heaven. [...] I am not the Christ, but I have been sent before him. He who has the bride is the bridegroom; the friend of the bridegroom, who stands and hears him, rejoices greatly at the bridegroom's voice; therefore this joy of mine is now full." (John 3:27-29)

In order to conclude this short development on Jesus' Call let us listen to him: "No one can come to me unless the Father who sent me draws him; and I will raise him up at the last day. It is written in the prophets, `And they shall all be taught by God.' Every one who has heard and learned from the Father comes to me." (John 6:44-45)

As witnesses and as leaders, we plan, we plan, but let us remember always our exact place: by the grace of God we facilitate the encounter; but God's Grace is Sovereign: "it depends not upon man's will or exertion, but upon God's mercy." (Romans 9:16)

Hearing Jesus' Call

Jesus Calls all Humanity

Jesus wants to call people to follow him from close up. In a more formal way it can also be termed, the "call for Holiness". Traditionally it is called as well the "second conversion", in the sense that one can well be a Christian, but lead a sort of a good reasonable life, good moral life, faithful to the weekly Mass, but from the Grace of God's point of view it is a lukewarm spiritual life: the relationship with Jesus has come to a halt. What does Jesus want us to do in order to awaken the grace of God in our brother's life? Jesus invites us to "facilitate the encounter", acting like a catalyst, witnessing to Jesus (telling others what he did to us).

Ask the Lord of the Harvest

One very important task we have is to answer Jesus' request to: "Ask the Lord of the harvest, therefore, to send out workers into his harvest field." (Matthew 9:38). At times that task can look frustrating. But this request remains a key request. Paradoxically (if you read the previous post) we seem not only to have a part to play in the "Call for Holiness", in the planning of it, but it is a totally different part from what we can think of: asking, in prayer, fervently, Jesus to send workers into his harvest field.

Having a personal relationship with Jesus, experiencing his love makes us burn with the desire to make him deeply known to the entire world. Would we just wait and watch things unfolding? Don't we have a role to play in Jesus' plan? Are we completely absent from Jesus' plan since: "it depends not upon man's will or exertion, but upon God's mercy." (Romans 9:16)? Oh no... we have to play our part in Jesus' plan, like Our Lady, and ask and pray fervently to obtain that Grace of Jesus' Calling to others. He asked us to do so.

Let us be united with Mary, like in Advent time, and pray and ask fervently for the Grace of God's mercy to reveal his son to many. It is a grace, it can be obtained, we just need to discover the most powerful way to obtain it.

Contemplating the one who, in her prayer, obtained for us the Messiah remains, in God's mind and plan the most powerful leaver.

Let us repeat with Mary, her prayer: send us oh Lord the Messiah, i.e. make many people discover Jesus, make Jesus knock at the door of many persons, giving them the grace of being enthused by spiritual life, by wanting to discover who is Jesus, have a relationship with Him, and embark on the journey with him. Mary's prayer, and Fire are so powerful. Let us unite with her. "Pray for us oh Mother of God"… obtain from Jesus for many many the grace of following him.

Easing the way for Jesus

Another aspect shouldn't be overlooked: People are not always ready to hear Jesus' call.

We are invited to take part in the Plan, as Jesus friends, like John the Baptist. We open the way for Jesus, facilitating for people the hearing of his call. Often his voice is so gentle, that the noise of our busy life won't allow us to hear him. The thick layer of all our desires, personal plans, work, family, does not allow us to hear his personal voice in our heart. Our lack of commitment and endeavour to many issues is not opening the way to Jesus to be heard.

At the end of the day we are faced with this truth: Jesus doesn't land on any soil. God always prepares the soil. We can take part in this preparation, and invite others to take part in it.

Abraham's three thresholds

Abraham is a good example of how God prepares the way in order for us to receive his precious gifts. Jesus' call is the most precious gift a human being can receive. Are you aware of that? But in order to value it, in order to receive it properly and make it bear fruit, the soil has to be prepared. God wanted to give Abraham the Promised land. The real Promised land for us is Jesus himself, to possess him, to be loved by him and love him, and serve him.

God could have given Abraham directly and immediately the promised land, but in fact he opened the way, ploughing the soil with powerful blades, so the soil can open in order to receive the Pearl of all pearls: the Promised land. He made Abraham go through 3 different thresholds.

1ˢᵗ Threshold: the freedom from my own land/tribe: He asks him to leave his land and go.

2ⁿᵈ Threshold: the freedom from the blood ties (son, parents, husband/wife): give me the most precious tie you have, give me your son Isaac. Do you prefer me, Jesus, above your mother, father, son, daughter, wife?

3ʳᵈ Threshold: the freedom and growth: you will go to Egypt, will work, grow, and take the goods (result of that effort). His descendants spent 430 years in Egypt, in order to cross that threshold.

It is only after these three thresholds that Abraham (Abraham descendants), would start the journey to the Holy Land, by Moses.

This example from the Old Testament, read in the Light of Jesus, helps us understand the role of John the Baptist, or better said: the first three thresholds that prepare the way for Jesus' call to-follow-him-from-close-up to be heard.

The three thresholds in the Gospel

We see that behaviour in Jesus with the Young Rich man. When he asks Jesus what he is supposed to do in order to reach Eternal life, Jesus doesn't start by saying: ok, good, excellent, I love you, come and follow me. On the contrary, Jesus checks the thresholds: have you been faithful to Moses' commandments?

The same thing happens in John's Gospel: we have a total of 6 steps in order to reach "opened heaven" (Jesus' side opened) i.e. God's Glory revealed in Jesus on the Cross. These 6 steps are 6 signs that John put, as steps, thresholds, in order to be purified, and become ready to enter the face to face with Jesus' Glory on the Cross, accessing heaven (i.e. his opened side). These signs could be divided into two lots: the first 3 and the following. What divides them is this second stage in Jesus' follower: crossing the sea, heading toward God himself, Holiness.

In this sense, the first three thresholds or signs mentioned by John are equivalent to Abraham's ones. Cana, the son of the military officer, the paralysed man.

Teresa of Avila's thresholds

Now, you might ask: do we have any proof in the Church's Spiritual Living Tradition of these thresholds?

– Of course, yes. If we look at St Teresa of Avila's masterpiece "The Interior Castle" we find the following: she paves the journey to "Union with Jesus" offering 7 different stages of growth; she calls them "Mansions". The surprising thing is that the "second conversion" happens only at the 4th Mansion. Entering into the living relationship with Jesus, the supernatural, starts only at that stage. One can neglect all what comes before. But in fact, the three mansions that precede are very important.

1- First, she invites the reader who is closer to Jesus and more especially the reader who reached that union with Jesus (see Seventh Mansion) never to forget to pray for the persons who are in the first mansions. She considers it as a very important act of Mercy not to forget the persons stuck in these stages.

2- Also, we need to study these three first mansions in order to understand the three different thresholds that the human being is called to cross. The most striking comment she makes, not only in my eyes, but in the eyes of a great man, Fr Marie Eugène (soon to become Blessed) is how she describes the Christian life of a person in the third mansion (i.e. right before discovering Jesus' personal call): she says that they lead a very reasonable life; you would say: they are "good Catholics". They have a good morality, they go to Church, they do good things, they help others,… All is there, but strangely, Jesus – the living Jesus – is not there! That note of hers, stressed again by Fr Marie Eugene in his masterpiece "I want to see God", should be enough to revolutionise the Church, people who think they are awake but in fact are perfectly dormant.

Summing up we can say:

1- it is very important to understand that Jesus' call is a grace, and even if a Grace of God can't be planned, controlled, we are strongly invited to pray to Jesus to give his grace. We need to obtain this grace. Acknowledging that it is a grace doesn't mean that we are helpless, it only means that we know our place: God's initiative is sovereign. Asking Mary to obtain that Grace is really the most powerful starting point.

2- Like John the Baptist, we need to prepare for our brothers the way for Jesus' call to be heard (bring them to Jesus' audio range). There are things to be done in order to be ready to hear. We will still have our freedom to say yes or no, but we will be more ready. See the three thresholds that Abraham and his descendants had to undergo in order to start their real journey to the Promised Land.

Getting ready to receive Jesus' Call

Q. You write that "comprehending the full picture of the Spiritual Journey is essential for each Christian who receives Jesus' call to follow Him". Does not every Christian receive Jesus' call to follow him?

A. A call is a call (see next chapter), it happens at a certain point in time. The fact that "all are called", doesn't mean that "all have yet received the call". The call is a personal act from Jesus, to a specific person, when the person is ready. We should remember the fact that the call is Jesus' initiative not ours. He says: "I am the one who calls you, not you".
Is that what you meant?

Of course, this is an important clarification that I didn't personally see for years. I was convinced, after Vatican II (see *Lumen Gentium*, "The Universal

Call to Holiness"[2]), that "all were called", but then, I realised that "a call is a call", and is not automatic, or to be taken for granted. This call has to enter in time, in the life of a person. And for that to happen, one should be ready. For instance, see how God sent John the Baptist to prepare the people of Israël to receive the Messiah.

Q. Is it possible some may never be ready i.e. never receive the call?

A. To speak plainly, I would say the following:
Theoretically the call is there in God's mind/project from day one, from the day he created us. He created us "at His Image and Likeness", He wanted us with Him, breathing His own life. So the initial design and built quality of the human being were meant to have him: being Holy, as God is, because we are made to share His Own life, and breath His own "oxygen".

But practically, I think that the call for Perfection is heard (/reaches us) in a palpable way when we are close to **a specific threshold**: having accomplished /fulfilled what should be done as it is described at the third Mansions of Teresa of Avila for example.

There are plenty of other Biblical examples that foster such a vision and understanding. **God always prepares us.**

1. All the Old Testament, 1800 years (Abraham) at least if not plenty more, is a preparation for humanity (the chosen people first) to receive God himself (the Messiah, Jesus, the Only begotten Son). He didn't send his Son to Adam immediately after his fall.

2. Again: when Jesus was ready to start his mission (at the age of 30) He didn't start immediately. God send a Prophet, the Greatest one, to pave the way for him, and "prepare" the people, through repentance and a first wash (John's Baptism).

3. Again, and again, when the Young Rich man asked him what to do in order to reach perfection, /Eternal life, Jesus didn't start by saying: follow

---

[2] See last chapter.

me. He showed us in His reply that preparation was needed: did you follow Moses Commandments?

In other words there is a clear pedagogy from God's part, in order to help us reach the Supernatural Grace of Jesus, the Personal relationship: the direct, personal call to follow him tightly.

I may add that if the young rich man had answered: "no, I didn't fulfil Moses commandments", he wouldn't be "ready" to "hear" a new Call, a call for Perfection.

Jesus doesn't cancel Moses Commandments, He brings Perfection to them, in Him. So, if what we can really do (with the General help of the Grace of God) is not done, how can we dare dream of higher realms? Total nonsense. Jesus said that faithfulness in "smaller things" will allow God one day to pass us unto greater things: "Well done, good and trustworthy servant, you have been trustworthy in a smaller things, I will put you in charge of greater things." (Matthew 25:21)

Some people might **object**: there are plenty of persons amongst the Gentiles (non Jews) in the Act of the Apostles and in the Gospel (the Samaritan lady) who didn't need any preparation. Well, it is not true: When Paul preached at the Assembly of Athens, almost nobody listened to him. They weren't ready. Some Fathers of the Church say that the Greeks were prepared by God through their Philosophers. Which is not wrong, but incomplete.

And **what about** the great sinners? Well: sin, falling very low, sometimes creates an amazing humility. See the Prodigal son's reflections while eating the pigs food (and compare them with the other son's reflections). Don't we use animal excrements to fertilise the soil ! Humility and real repentance are the best preparations to receive Jesus' Call and Grace. But still, repentance is a long journey of rehabilitation. Even St Paul says that after his powerful conversion he needed 3 years of rehabilitation (see Galatians) and purification.

I humbly think that often we tend to abuse the Grace of God, thinking that we have the right to receive everything. Jesus himself (God) doesn't through

15

the pearls to the pigs (pigs were considered as an impure animal). But in fact, this is a spoiled child behaviour. Certainly He obtained for us everything (Salvation) on the Cross, but the clear teaching of the Bible shows that for each new step one has to be ready.

Matthew's Call (Caravaggio – Rome)

So, all in all, we need to do what each step requires, in order to get to the threshold with the following step.

See the journey of the People of God in the Desert. They reach a point where they break the Covenant with God in a grave way, they don't TRUST Him when He says: "go and fight the 7 tribes, you will win". What is the consequence? 38 years of purification, until all the generation that was able to fight dies. This lesson alone should make us think. Poor us. (see the clear allusion to these 38 years in John Chapter 5, the healing of the paralysed man.)

If, from God's part, Salvation is ready and available to us, from our part (the receiving end) we need **to get ready**to receive it, and this goes step by step, like when you build a huge house. You start with the Foundations, then you go for the ground floor and so forth.

Even if the Plan of the house is ready and clear in God's mind, we have to undergo the building operations, step by step. Some people think that if they want to burn the stages in between this is possible. Let them think that. You don't put a New Wine in old skins. We collaborate in the operation of our own salvation, we are co-builders. Some people believe in magic, they think that since Jesus did everything on the Cross then everything is already achieved in us. Not at all. Baptism is a Seed, and the Seed needs to become the biggest tree of the garden. Would this happen magically? People who follow Satan's inspirations do like the magical easy way. All the three temptations that we see in the Gospel (when Jesus is tempted) are about doing something magically, in an easy way, without the use of our freedom and will, collaborating, through time.

We want to be like puppets, we like that route (the devil's route) of negative passiveness. We want everything and NOW! We want Him to move us and direct us like dead-puppets. We present the resignation of our will and freedom.

The **Call for Perfection** follows the laws of construction… or the biological laws of growth. The Grace of God needs our collaboration.
God created us without asking for our permission. He won't save us, though, without our collaboration.

Comment: "For me this article is powerful. Subtle yet says so much! Only two things in the beginning made me wonder but as I read on it becomes clear.

There seems to be a general assumption amongst Catholics that we are already sort of holy (sinless) because we are in a state of grace (through the Sacrament of Confession). There is also a misunderstanding that it is enough just by avoiding sins that are listed by the Church. Sometimes there is a lack of consideration with regards to our words/actions/thoughts that are wrong by conscience or hurtful to others as long as they are not listed as a sin. So, in a way holiness becomes ticking the boxes of sin or no sin and also relying on the "works/missions" we do. This is a shame because it is to our conscience that the still small voice of God speaks in order to transform us into the children of His intention. I sometimes wonder if that's why Protestants mistakenly accuse Catholics of relying on our own good works for salvation.

The path of holiness is a difficult one. It requires a lot of energy, commitment and pain as you mentioned and sadly not many are willing. There is I think a preference to believe in the easier option (as though there's one!) of our own good works/missions but it is only an illusion. Perhaps that's why there is a constant focus on certain favourites such as abortion/gay marriage. Not that these aren't important but if we use these as a way of deflecting from our inner self, then it works against the growth of our spiritual lives. For it is an absolute necessity in the path to holiness to look inside of oneself." (H.T.)

Lectio Divina and vocation

This chapter[3] on "*Lectio* and Vocation" is motivated by a frequent and painful observation: the question of what one will become in life, of what form one's life will take is often asked. Religious consecration? Marriage? Celibacy? Commitment? And so on… We suffer greatly from this preoccupation. And, conversely, we give much less importance to our daily faithfulness to God. In fact, we do *invert* the order of our preoccupations; and this does us harm. We are able to go on a retreat just to find out what we should do in life, but that we should have such great "anxiety" concerning our faithfulness to God in day-to-day life is a thought that never really touches us.

The aim, then, of this fourth paragraph is to propose an important point of discernment, so that we may better live on a daily basis and bring our life to fulfilment. We will come to perceive that there is actually only one call: to follow Christ, to know Him – no matter in what form this will be incarnated. Indeed this call resembles a tree; and *Lectio* is one of the strongest means to make it grow. On the other hand, the incarnation of our vocation (marriage, religious consecration, etc…) appears in its time like a *ripened fruit* of this unique tree of faithfulness to God.

To help us in our reflection to determine our practical vocation, let us take the example of the tree. If we do not have much knowledge of the variety of trees that exist, and if we see a tiny little tree, we cannot say of what sort it is: an orange tree or an apple tree… We will be able to determine what kind of tree it is by seeing its fruit. The same is true of a vocation. It appears on the tree in the form of a ripened fruit and tells us what kind of tree it is. If we see an apple, we will know that it is an apple tree. So, instead of asking ourselves, and torturing our minds, instead centring our prayers on this preoccupation, we should apply our attention to watering the tree. In fact, if we spend our time asking questions instead of watering the tree, we will be stopping the realisation of our vocation.

---

[3] This chapter is taken from the book : Jean Khoury, "Lectio Divina at the School of Mary" (see on Amazon).

Lectio is offered as one of the best means for helping the tree to grow. Through it, we may directly know, when the time comes and not before, what we are destined to be. God could indeed reveal this to us, but this knowledge might lead us to go too quickly, to miss some important steps and to invert the priorities. This is often why He hides this knowledge from us for a long time, and sometimes right up to the last limit. He is then using a pedagogical method that teaches us to attach ourselves to what is essential: Himself, day after day. Because what good is it finally to know what we are to become if we are unable to listen to the Lord on a daily basis. Our fidelity in the accomplishment of our vocation will not last.

Let us consider this more closely.

1. Vocation

a) What is a vocation?
The etymological meaning of vocation - from the Latin *vocare* - is "call". In order for a call to exist there needs to be someone who calls and someone who is called and a relationship between the two. The Gospel is neither an ideology nor a comfortable nest. It is a living and personal relationship with Christ today. A relationship supposes movement and progression. Christ is not static. He advances and invites us to follow Him. His call is a personal one; He comes to each human being, looks at Him profoundly at a given moment in his life, reveals His Life to him and offers him His hand, inviting him to walk in his footsteps.

b) Christ is the Way
Christ is our basic vocation. The particular vocation (marriage, religious consecration, celibacy, a particular mission as a lay-person, etc…) is the manner in which each of us is going to live out his or her basic vocation; in this sense the particular vocation is secondary. On account of our deformed inclination, we have the tendency to inverting things and we give more importance to the particular vocation than to the basic one of following Christ. But following Christ step by step - no matter what our situation may be - is the heart of our life. Christ is our Way.

c) We are all called

All of us are called to follow Christ; this is our basic vocation. On the cross He died for all people, and so everyone is called to follow Him. *Lectio* will be the royal way to listen to the One who is calling us, and He will teach us to become like Him by following in his footsteps.

Saint John, in chapter 6, contains statements that may make us doubt about our being chosen or called by the Lord[4]. How can we explain this complex problem that, if we like it or not, plunges us into the divine plan concerning predestination? All have been tormented by this problem, those with the greatest renown and the most humble.

We actually find the answer in the fact that God calls every person, since He wants the Salvation of all and died on the Cross for everyone. So I can have no doubt about God's calling me. In other words, the sun can only shine, and if there are some dark or doubtful clouds (my own thoughts) they do not come from Him. Above these clouds, the sun is always shining. In fact, everything is determined by my answer. I can answer by myself, taking myself as the starting point and constructing my own way of following Christ. But I can also ask the Holy Spirit to help me listen to the one calling me, and to follow Him step by step at his rhythm and by doing his will. This is of course much more demanding, but, in this way, the call is accomplished. Otherwise, I think that I am responding, but in reality my actions are coming from my "ego". I direct the answer to the call. At the end, I will say to the Lord: "I preached your Name, and did this and that for you…", and He will rely: "Go away from me; I do not know you."

The Lord is the one who addresses the call, He gives the strength to accomplish it day after day, in the manner He chooses, and it is He who realises its accomplishment.

We enter *Lectio* with the idea of discovering some plans, to get a general view of our life or our future as related to God's project. But this is impossible because we are called to change. We cannot know what we will

---

[4] "All that the Father gives to me will come to me" (Jn 6:37); "No one is able to come to me, if the Father who sent me does not draw him" (Jn 6:44); "No one is able to come to me, if it has not been given him from my Father" (Jn 6:65).

become, so how could we understand an entire project or orientation? Divine pedagogy does not work like this, it does not lead us with sudden revelations; it advances progressively. Our human haste more often than not obstructs his work with our own. We have the task of discovering, day after day, what we should understand and do in daily life. He has His projects. Our intelligence has the task of executing them.

d) Conditions for answering the call
One may only decide on a vocation freely and after being well informed. It is therefore necessary to acquire a minimum of experience, of acquaintanceship with Christ, and to be freed by Him in order to be able to choose. Maturity is therefore necessary, as well as our being rooted in Him.

e) The Vocation, following Christ, a tree
A vocation is then like a tree. On the one hand, it needs to grow and, on the other, seeing the fruits, helps to determine what kind of tree it is.

i) The growth of the tree
As we have seen in Part Two, Christ, through *Lectio*, becomes flesh in one "mouthful" at a time. Each day a part of us is renewed. The new man slowly takes his place and grows, while the old man perishes. One zone after another of our will is daily renewed, recreated. Christ truly grows in us. He slowly takes possession of us, transforms us and directs us. He comes to life in us. The Kingdom of God is like a seed, the smallest of all the seeds, and it becomes a big tree. This is the growth of Christ in us.

ii) The vocation is the fruit of the tree
One cannot determine a vocation, i.e. it is impossible to say what kind of fruit our tree will bear until it has reached its full size. The growth of the tree, of Jesus in us, which receives great sustenance from *Lectio*, allows us to determine our particular vocation. So let us see how *Lectio* is integrated in the discernment of our vocation! We recognise a vocation by its fruit. Faithfulness to God, by listening to him each day, through the solid friendship based on His living Word, strongly helps the tree of vocation to grow (whatever kind it may be). Then discernment becomes easy; sometimes it is harvested as a mature fruit, just in time! Moreover, *Lectio*, since it forms maturity and the capacity of making decisions, leads us also

to the fundamental choice of truly becoming friends of Christ, thanks to a personal acquaintance.

2. The call and *Lectio*

a) *Lectio* permits us to walk along this road

In *Lectio* Christ has the first place and I have the second. He speaks and I listen. The danger exist that *Lectio*, instead of being a time of listening, becomes a moment of decision making for me, where I appropriate the Word for myself. When I do this, I take the place of Christ, and I am no longer listening. For this reason, the Holy Spirit helps me to listen, to adjust my relationship with Christ by giving him the first place.

There is also a risk a calling oneself, of deciding by oneself the meaning of the Word of the day. But the movement of listening is just the opposite: He begins to speak. The invocation of the Holy Spirit puts us in our right place. By daily listening to Christ, who calls us to follow Him, we find the steps to take. And so we walk in Christ's footsteps.

b) Practising *Lectio* implies a commitment

Lectio also supposes that one is committed to Christ. The exercise of *Lectio* is particularly demanding, and as long as one is not fully devoted in one's heart to searching for the truth and to meeting Christ, it is difficult to listen.

3. *Lectio* and accompanying vocations

Evidently, in order to discern a vocation really well it is necessary to listen to the Lord every day. It is not possible to say that one has a vocation if one does not practise *Lectio*. That would be tempting the Lord[5]. Each person who

---

[5] When the devil tempted the Lord in the desert "he brought him to Jerusalem, and set him on the pinnacle of the temple, and said to him, `If the Son you are of God, cast yourself down from here, for it has been written: 'To His messengers He will give charge concerning you, to watch over you,' and: 'On hands they shall bear you up, lest at any time you dash your foot against a stone.'" But Jesus replied: "'It has been said, You shall not tempt the Lord your God.'"(Lk 4:9-12). Progressing in one's vocation without the support of *Lectio* is like throwing oneself down from the pinnacle of the Temple and saying: "The angels of the Lord will save me, since I am God's child!" It is impossible to advance in one's vocation without the substantial help of *Lectio*; this would simply be "tempting God".

is called or who wishes to discern, according to his or her possibilities, should practise *Lectio*. Nevertheless, it is evident that if the Lord calls, or seems to call, (and He calls everyone to follow Him), it is not normal to allow only a few possibilities for Him to speak to us. Tempting the Lord manifests a lack of wisdom. If one continues to be engrossed in a thousand different things and states: The Lord is calling me; if He does this, He knows what He is doing and He will be able to direct me in another way if He wishes. But no, the Lord expects us to choose with our will and our intellect. Without us he cannot and will not act. If He does so as an exception He does so in mercy; but normally we come to see that we are inverting the values, and that as a consequence we need to change the rhythm of our lives, even if it is at a price. Of course, it is good to talk with a priest or experienced guide. But sooner or later our life needs to progress toward the recognition that *Lectio* needs to be done on a daily basis.

Many people are called and many end up losing their call. This does not mean that the Lord has stopped calling them (the Lord does not take back his gifts), but we have regressed to the point of losing what we had gained. A call is like a small seed that must become a big tree. If the seed is not watered, nourished and taken care of, it cannot reach maturity. When the first storm or temptation comes, or another voice, it gives way. People trample on it and the call seems to be definitively lost. Now, *Lectio* allows the seed to grow, protecting it like a guard tower against everything and everyone. The humble person, who practises *Lectio* everyday, has incredible strength; he or she is able to confront all the contradictions through the grace coming from the daily encounter with Christ who speaks, consoles and securely guides him or her.

Sometimes people think that a retreat for discernment is sufficient. But before or after the retreat they neglect to be faithful to daily *Lectio*. If we have discerned that the Lord is calling us and suppose that we have been "put on the right track", that "all will go well", we are fooling ourselves, because we have to live faithfully every day!

When mediation blurs

Sometimes certain people do not really discover their vocation: they are oriented; they receive counselling and are directed; but, although they "advance", a certain distance still separates them from Christ. The vivifying encounter with Christ does not occur "freely", and when this happens these people do not listen to the call directly. Now, *Lectio* puts us into direct contact with Christ. He is the vocation of each Baptised Christian; He gives strength and energy; He seduces and draws; He convinces and commits. All mediation serves this relationship, and ought to promote it. But when the mediation is self-interested – often unconsciously - when spiritual direction becomes a projection onto the person being accompanied, a screen is erected which breaks the relationship instead of furthering it. In this case, *Lectio* itself may be compromised.

4. The call

We have made a clear distinction between the call to follow Christ and how this call will be realised, whether in marriage, consecrated life, or celibate life. And the role *Lectio* plays in the growth and discernment of all types of vocations is evident. But in the following paragraphs we will talk specifically about its role in consecrated life and in the priesthood, and for those who are candidates or feel the call to religious life or to the priesthood.

a) *Lectio* and consecrated life

As we have said above, it is easy for us to deduce what may happen to a vocation that is only partially realised by someone who has entered religious life. The plant - Christ in that person - has not yet reached its full maturity, and is still far from that goal. If *Lectio* is abandoned, as we have seen above, the vocation will slowly wither. This is easy to see in the lives of religious and priests. But when they practise *Lectio*, their faith is vibrant and alive. Their faith is strong. They put up resistance against worldliness, which tries in every possible way to invade them. Their mind is very clear, the light of Christ illumines them and visibly consoles them.

On the other hand, those who neglect *Lectio*, or only practise it occasionally, poorly or too quickly, see their faith decline and the world take over the field of their hearts. Their consecration greatly suffers. It is true to say that their faith is proportional to their practice of real *Lectio*.

b) *Lectio* and the call to priesthood

The same thing may be said of those who are called to the priesthood. This is so because the priest is called to sanctity, and the saintlier he is, the more docile an instrument he is in the hands of God, the more God acts in him and works through him. And *Lectio* is the best way to prepare the 'instrument', to render it ever more docile to the light of God. Of course, the future priest receives special graces that lead him to a particular type of intimacy with God so that he may better understand his brethren and serve them. So *Lectio* is even more necessary - if we may say this - for the future priest. If it bears fruit of sanctification in the future religious, it also gives to the future priest graces of deeper understanding of Scripture. Indeed, the priest's task is that of a privileged friend of Christ, who understands His plans and collaborates with Him.

5. Conclusion

We can conclude by stating this: We should, in reality, avoid reversing the order of our preoccupations. Faithfulness to God in daily life is more important than our care for the future. Certainly, we must be concerned about the future for otherwise we would do nothing. But the preoccupation and the anxiety that it creates need to be directed toward the truth in daily faithfulness. If not we will be trying out "magic" solutions. They may appear easy, quick and accessible, and so one prefers to go on just one retreat to figure out what to do with one's life. But the faithfulness to God through *Lectio*, before and after the retreat, does not really seem important, because we consider it as being less "dramatic". But we are listening to God Himself by doing *Lectio*! And God is not an object we can manipulate; He is a living and intimate being! One might also open a page of the Bible by chance, hoping to find an answer. But a more demanding solution like the faithfulness to listening to the Lord each day may seem to us to be too high a price to pay, since it implies giving oneself!

St. Teresa's Conversion: the Meaning of her Life

St. Teresa's 'second conversion'[6] remains central in her life and teaching to the point that in the her autobiography she draws a golden divide: the time before her second conversion and the time after it. Before her conversion it's her life alone and afterwards it's Jesus' life in her. This momentous event in her life is so important that it gives meaning to all that will follow: her powerful spiritual growth, the foundation of the first reformed monastery, not to mention the foundation of many other monasteries. Throughout her life and writings she will then repeat the key lesson she learned from her conversion. We often hear her talking about her sins, for example, and God's mercy towards her. This is not a figure of speech or a pious attitude, or random words: it is the simple truth. Her conversion is, in fact, what we call a 'second conversion', bearing in mind that she is, of course, already a Christian and a nun. This conversion concerns going from a normal 'traditional' Christian life to entering into a day-to-day personal relationship with the Risen Lord.

When she is thirty-nine years old she experiences the said conversion, having first entered the Monastery of the Incarnation in Avila (Spain) at only twenty years of age. It should be borne in mind, here, that the two reasons for which she entered would not be sufficient nowadays for a girl's acceptance in a monastery: first, she had a very dear friend of hers already inside this particular monastery and secondly, she feared committing mortal sin. Why mortal sin? She had a keen awareness that she was attractive and entertaining; in fact, many of her cousins were attracted to her. She also was aware that she was weak and feared falling into mortal sin. Of course, there are plenty of other implicit reasons: one of them is her great devotion to Our Lady whom she adopted as a mother after the death of her own mother. In fact, the Carmelite order is known as the Order 'of Our Lady'.

On the surface, however, her religious life seemed good. She was a spiritual person, observant, faithful to religious life. But seen from the perspective of the heart or the emotions, she was failing to belong totally to Christ-The-

---

[6] This chapter is taken from the book: Jean Khoury, "The Foundations of Spiritual Life According to St. Teresa of Avila" (see in Amazon).

Groom. She was not, curiously, totally aware of this lack. This might seem strange considering her way of life where she used to meet people in the parlour and talk to them about prayer, mental prayer at that – she was capable of entertaining people concerning the spiritual life for hours! Revealingly her emotions were not totally in the hands of Christ, liking as she did to talk and entertain, clinging thereby to these relationships. Indubitably no sin is being committed here, especially according to today's criteria. But Christ does not look at our outward behaviour, rather He sees into our heart, and it's our heart that He is waiting for! One has to say that the Lord had been patient with her – almost twenty years – then He took pity on her, wanting to change her. Blessed be Him Eternally for His Mercy!

The modern reader, consequently, would not see a problem with what she was doing since, when looked at superficially, she is not committing any sin. We know, as well, that she would never have sinned knowingly and deliberately. It must be remembered that it is for this reason that she entered the monastery: to avoid mortal sin. So if there is no apparent sin, where is the problem? What kind of 'conversion' does she need? After all, she leads a good monastic life and through it she glorifies God! The fact remains, however, that she was blind until the Lord, with His merciful Grace, showed her from within, in her heart and emotions, what was lacking, what she was not giving to Him. Her heart in fact was divided, even worse, it was spread thin, veering outwards rather than being focused inwards on God. The relationships she was having, talking about God, were certainly above-board, but at the emotional level, her heart was geared outwards, her emotions being involved with them. Seen from Christ-The-Groom point of view, she was not totally His, certainly not in all her emotions.

Being in the monastery does not mean that one automatically praises only God. One needs to be with Christ in order to receive all the graces He wants to give us and to grow until we reach union with Him and the fullness of charity. Monastic life does not mean only refraining from sinning and fulfilling somehow or other the duties of our state of life. It goes infinitely deeper than that. Seen from this perspective, then, her vision of Christian life, monastic life and of her duties was impoverished. Her understanding of Christ was limited, especially about what He was seeking and waiting for from her, what he expects from each one of us: all of our heart given to him

- our emotional heart included. Today one would use the word 'eros' to characterise this, recognising the second lower half of our heart that we often keep for the love of human beings.

St. Teresa often takes the time to explain in different places in her writings this turning point in her life. In fact, we can only understand her life and achievements through it, for it will trigger a powerful spiritual life, an abundance of graces. The Lord was patiently waiting for this change to happen, to no avail. She was just not seeing it! This is why, afterward, she felt the constant urge to mention it and to sing the mercies of the Lord who had not only waited for her patiently, but who showed her what He wanted from her most gently: all of her, all her emotions, every fibre of her being, all for Him and Him only! It is only after doing so that the torrent of his graces was triggered! And then, a new life started, another Teresa started to emerge, the Teresa 'of Jesus'! From that moment on, as she states in her *Life*, it is the story of the life of Jesus in her. (*Life* 23,1)

On the one hand I am sure that for the modern reader the difference is minute between the way she was leading her life and what Christ wanted from her. On the other hand, one has to sincerely admit that for us (including consecrated people) if we apply her criterium (giving everything including our emotional heart), very few would be 'saved'! Or, in other words: if we follow her reading and understanding of the light that Jesus showed her and apply it to everybody, many things in the Church would have to change! St. Teresa greatly emphasises this point and it is to be feared that it might be easily overlooked. According to the criteria of Christian moral life, we all agree that she was not committing any sin, not even a fault against her state of life! Indeed, filtered through the eyes of moral theology, there is no formal sin. But what we learn from her is that all Christian life does not lie in moral theology. God sees our heart, but unfortunately, we do not understand ourselves! St. Augustine says that we search for God in the 'external world' while God searches for us 'internally'! Teresa was unconsciously searching for God outside of herself, in the relationships she was having. No formal sin was committed but she was ignorant, especially of God's ways and how to reach Him, or better said: how to be reached by God, how to really open the door to the heart in order to receive the abundance of his graces and then grow until union with Him is attained. The Saint, who in that period felt deeply in tune with the St. Augustine of the *Confessions*, thus describes the decisive day of her mystical experience: *and... a feeling of the presence of God would come over me unexpectedly, so that I could in no wise doubt either that he was within me, or that I was wholly absorbed in him. (Vida, 10, 1)." (Pope Benedict XVI *Catechesis, on St. Teresa*)[7]

These are very important questions and the common answers to them do not give evidence of the essence of the Gospel. Therefore, if we continue to impoverish Christian life this way, St. Teresa's life will become in-comprehensible to us, as categorically will be our understanding of Christian life in toto. We need fewer superficial criteria and more thorough filters, or rather a more refined filter: Spiritual Theology, or the teaching of the Church on Spiritual life. There is a fundamental reason for this: it reaches the core of our Christian life. It shows the real goal of the Christian life, that is, union with God; it shows us the decisive step to take to reach it, hardly mentioned today, that is, giving Jesus the lower part of our heart (see also next chapter) and finally, as we will see later, it shows, in practice, the means to reach the goal through practising virtues and the Prayer of the Heart. It is not clear, as yet in today's day and age, whether by and large we have or have not given our heart, our emotions, to the Lord!

The Lord Himself is a prime exemplar of using various circumstances and means to shed his light in St. Teresa and show her what He wanted from her, what she was denying him! As mentioned above, she was reading (during Lent of 1554) the *Confessions* of St. Augustine and was struck by the beautiful passage where he mentions his misery and error in choosing the wrong direction while searching for God: exteriorly instead of interiorly:

---

[7] What light does St. Teresa's conversion sheds on today's state of Theology? God asks us at least two questions when, through her conversion, He challenges our way of viewing Theology today.
- Does today's teaching in moral theology speak in a practical way about 'Union with God'? No, it definitely does not.
- Does Christian Moral life still seem to consist only in the fact of avoiding sin, that is. being in a state of grace?
Indeed it does.

Too late did I love You, O Fairness, so ancient, and yet so new! Too late did I love You! For behold, You were within, and I without, and there did I seek You; I, unlovely, rushed heedlessly among the things of beauty You made. You were with me, but I was not with You. Those things kept me far from You, which, unless they were in You, were not. You called, and cried aloud, and forced open my deafness. You gleamed and shine, and chase away my blindness. You exhaled odours, and I drew in my breath and do pant after You. I tasted, and do hunger and thirst. You touched me, and I burned for Your peace.
When I shall cleave unto You with all my being, then shall I in nothing have pain and labour; and my life shall be a real life, being wholly full of You.
(Saint Augustine, *Confessions*, X, 27, 38)

Reading this passage during Lent of 1554 Teresa was touched, and it proved a decisive moment posing many questions as it did: where is God? Is He outside or within his creatures? Can He be found through an intellectual quest? Is He in one's relationships with others (one can easily call this 'love of neighbour', to legitimise it)! Where is one's heart? The Gospel says *your heart will be where your treasure is* (Matthew 6:21)! And who is our Treasure? We do not see God, He is unknown to us, but our real Treasure, this immensely deep Well, those abundant Living Waters is Christ! And Christ is the Groom, the Beloved of our heart! Where is Christ? Is He outside? This is what St. Teresa actually thought! The result is a dramatic change touching the very core of her being: He is not to be found outside, but He is inside of her, in the depths of her heart. She will search for him yes, but now will do so in her heart of hearts. Henceforth she will learn never to leave him alone in her heart! It is through this reading, then, that she receives one of the few electric jolts the grace of God will use to return her to Himself. This one will make her become altogether aware of the greatness of man and of her former error of judgment! Yes the man is great, immense; she will later get to discover the inner beauty that the soul will regain by growing in Christ! The baptised person, in fact, is like a living and walking Tabernacle! Now, not as before when all her energy and emotions were outward bound, the grace of God used St. Augustine's passage to turn Teresa powerfully toward God dwelling within her.

The other jolt given by the grace of God was when her eyes met the eyes of Jesus! This was worth all the treasures of the world. Having contact with Jesus' eyes seemed indefinable! In His mercy, Christ used a very small polychrome statue of Christ at the Pillar to pour forth his Grace, to touch her and talk to her – with all the pain that He had suffered because of her and for her. But mainly it was his gaze that touched her. Christ, at the pillar with his hands tied to it, covered in wounds, turning his head toward her, looking at her, into her very eyes! When the two gazes met – by the grace of God – the beauty of Christ, his love for her, moved her soul, her heart, deeply – moved everything within her. Everything seemed to vanish, all the external attachments she had sought, all that she had undertaken, all the beauties of creation disappeared in an instant in the face of the power of his Love, of his Gaze, of his Beauty! This beauty, capable of dramatically changing the entire world, was directed toward herself! This Beauty acted – by the Mercy of God – as a very powerful magnet! And this only was enough!

Christ himself, now, would accomplish and complete the inner conversion. This would be the final jolt. One day, He would speak to St. Teresa, summoning her not to be busy with the outer world but to direct her 'busyness' only towards him. He seems to say these words to her: 'Stop speaking to human beings!' He wanted her totally for himself! Christ is absolute in his dealings with us! He wants it all! There are no half-measures! He has an immense thirst, a divine thirst to give himself to us, but in order to do so, He needs us to be entirely - absolutely entirely - his. Not even a drop of our being cannot be his! Christ's love is radical, but He fills us in a royal way! His way of giving himself to us, the abundance of His graces, the beauty of the gift of Himself are beyond our wildest imagination! Only by putting Teresa's belief to the test will the unbeliever see the truth of it - he will definitely never repent doing so.

We can now understand the indisputable reason why St. Teresa repeatedly underlines in her writings the divine equation of spiritual life: if you want to receive Him totally, in all the royal abundance of the Gift of Himself, you need to give him everything, to entrust everything into his hands!

This decision can be taken right now, by the Grace of God:

'Lord I am weak,
Lord my heart is spread outward busy with many things
but I would like to belong to you totally,
I offer you all that is dear to me
like Abraham offered you his only child,
I put it in your hands,
and then I offer myself to you, entirely to you.
Make of me whatever you want.'

Sadly, it must be recognised, that three minutes after we offer ourselves, we take back our freedom. This is why this act of offering oneself would be repeated various times afterwards in Teresa's life. We too should often repeat it, because God created us capable of free will and therefore capable of offering ourselves to him. Amazingly every minute of free will is an equal opportunity to love Him again and again and to be loved by Him in return.

One cannot fathom how much this gift of ourselves to Him has 'power' over him. It is like a huge magnet that attracts and seduces Christ. He is encouraged to abandon himself to unheard of things: He pours out his Grace in abundance!

All this, however, remains a matter of experience. It has to be checked out first hand!

The Call for Holiness for Married People

For Married people there is a "call for Holiness"; but a "call" means that in married life there is a time spent "before the call" and another "after the call".

We all know that holiness can be achieved through all forms of life: being single, married, priest, consecrated (monk, religious, …). By the Grace of Jesus, all forms of life can be transformed into means to achieve holiness. In saying that, we refer to the Council *Vatican II*, more precisely to chapter V of the Document called: *"Lumen Gentium"*[8]: "The universal **CALL** to holiness in the Church". Here are some quotes:

- *"in the Church, everyone whether belonging to the hierarchy, or being cared for by it, is **called** to holiness, according to the saying of the Apostle: "For this is the will of God, your sanctification"."* (LG 39)
- *"The followers of Christ are **called** by God, not because of their works, but according to His own purpose and grace. They are justified in the Lord Jesus, because in the baptism of faith they truly become sons of God and sharers in the divine nature. In this way they are really made holy. Then too, by God's gift, they must hold on to and complete in their lives this holiness they have received."* (LG 40)
- *"it is evident to everyone, that all the faithful of Christ of whatever rank or status, are **called** to the fullness of the Christian life and to the perfection of charity"* (LG 40)
- As a consequence: *"all the faithful of Christ are **invited** to strive for the holiness and perfection of their own proper state. Indeed they have an **obligation** to so strive"* (LG 42)

A Call is a Call

Recently I was pondering on the issue of the "obligation to strive for holiness" and noticed that, very easily, the "call" can be transformed into a natural "obligation" for all. The difference between a unique "supernatural

---

[8] See last chapter.

call" from Christ to a specific person, and an "obligation for all Baptised people", is huge and should be explained.

As you can see, the word **"call"** is used various times in the quotes. We, obviously, have the same expression in all other documents of the Church (ordinary teaching of the Popes and the Bishops, the Catechism,…).

Let us first consider the reality of the "**Call** to holiness", all its aspects and implications:

1- The call has **a goal**: to start the journey toward holiness is something.

2- A "call" is **a grace**. A "grace" is by definition "free", and depends totally on the freedom of God.

3- It is a grace received **at a certain point** in our life (not before), according to the wisdom of God, and in the form and intensity His wisdom sees and decides. Placed in time.

4- The "call" involves **Jesus** Himself, **directly**, personally.

5- The "call" means that Jesus has **the priority** and the initiative in calling us: as He says in the Gospel: I called you, you didn't invite yourself.

6- The "call" involves the direct, efficient and transformative Action of the **Holy Spirit**.

7- It involves, at the receiving end, from the faithful **the following acts**: sitting down, listening, pondering, discerning, responding to this Call/grace, using the means involved in this call, in order to be able to respond to it on the long term.

Baptism: The normal call, for instance to priesthood or to religious life, means that the person was first baptised, confirmed… had a "normal active Christian life"… then, at a certain point in their life, they heard this "Call" from Jesus. (Sometimes the "call" grows progressively like a gentle dawn. But it is still a personal "call" from Jesus.)

Marriage: In a parallel way, we may say that a married couple receives the Sacrament of Marriage and lives with it normally. Then, I do believe that for the couple as well, they can receive the "call" for holiness, either early in their married life, or later… often one of the members of the couple (husband or wife), rarely both (it would be a huge grace).

As you can see the "call" is not something "automatic", or "spontaneous", or "done at will", even if we are baptised and are supposed to strive to holiness. Being baptised doesn't necessarily mean that we **heard Jesus' Call** or that we hear it every day. Baptism can be neglected, as a dormant seed in the earth of our being, waiting for the "right moment" to wake up.

What I would like to point out to is that when we say that "marriage is a way for holiness", we might sort of forget all the dynamics of the "Call". In fact, before a certain moment in their life, the married couple doesn't necessarily have that call (both, or each separately). Potentially it is there, included within the sacrament (of Marriage), like it is the case for the Sacrament of Baptism, but it is there "dormant", waiting for Jesus' visit to the couple or to one of them. In one word: the married couple needs to receive/hear the "call" for holiness, and, in the meantime, they might have things to achieve before being able to **"hear"** the call.
"all are called to Holiness": in fact, we can understand that statement in two ways at least:
1- Either: "there is a call that all will receive one day". The "call" is potentially present, but activated only at a certain point in time.
2- Or: "all are already in a journey that leads to holiness". It means: being married is a way for holiness. The "call" is actively present from day one (baptism, marriage).

There is a considerable difference between the two, even if that for many persons the two are not opposed. What might be **"new"** to many of us is to become aware that: before, during or after marrying, we'll receive a "call for Holiness". So we need to be prepared for it.

It is not because we are married, that we are supposed (without a "call") to reach holiness. We need to "hear the call", we need to discern the "call".

You might object: – does this means that many couples, married in the Church, can just stay married in a state of apathy, without doing anything for their holiness? Does this make, within married people, two categories?
– Well, theoretically and mostly practically: "yes". We are all baptised, but not all of us did receive a direct personal call to holiness. Do you see what I mean?

It is not because I am baptised that I am supposed to be on my way for holiness. No. On the contrary. One day, I will receive the call for holiness, the call to follow Jesus.

Notice: all my life before the call is not empty or without meaning. It is just a different life that deserves all its respect and requires as well from us to do many things. Before receiving the call for holiness there is a call for maturity, a preparation. Remember the rich young man. When he meets Jesus, he asks him: "what am I supposed to do in order to reach eternal life (instead of "eternal life" you may put: "holiness", "perfection")?" In His reply, Jesus didn't start mentioning "holiness"! On the contrary, He wanted to ensure that the foundations of this person are sound; so He said to him: **did you fulfil Moses Commandments?** In these commandments we have all the foundations of human life. Among the 10 Commandments one can extract the duties of the husband and wife within Marriage.

This doesn't mean YET that, by receiving the Sacrament of Marriage, there is a "call" for holiness. First things first. Shocking maybe, for many, but true. Jesus didn't start to speak about holiness. He said: "did you fulfil Moses commandments?". We perfectly know that these commandments are not the call for holiness/perfection. They are the foundation.

In the series of Signs of the Journey that leads us to the Union with Jesus, saint John doesn't start with holiness. He starts by offering us Mary, the New Even, Mother of our Faith (John 2), then he shows us how Jesus heals the son of a man (and indirectly the man himself) (John 4), then Jesus heals a paralysed man who doesn't have any friend in the world, and can't do anything in his life (John 5). So Jesus works first on 1- Our Roots 2- our close relationships (son, father, partner..) 3- our work, action in the world..

It is only after these fundamental steps that Jesus starts to do greater things, call us, and make us "cross the Sea" (John 6).

I hope you can see the difference between these steps in spiritual life and what the "call for holiness" means and involves.

What Is Our Goal in Life?

Originally, according to the early tradition of the Church, St. John the Evangelist was the only person called Theologian. Why so? It is often said because he was the only one who from within the Trinity was able to tell us about Christ's Divinity. In fact he starts his Gospel not only by stating the Lord's Divinity, but by a close contemplation of the Triune God. In the early times, to Theologise was to be admitted in the Trinity, dwelling in the Son, contemplating the Father, in the Communion of the Holy Spirit. In this sense Theology is a guide that leads us to the highest experience, it brings us back to our original state, as we were created and redeemed by God[9].

Some other authors of the early centuries, like Dionysius the Areopagite, considered all the authors of the books of the Bible as Theologians. They are all bearers of God's Word who guides us in our journey toward Him.

Let us go back to The Theologian, St. John the Evangelist and see how he understood Theology. And let us start with one of the most mysterious books of the New Testament, the book of Revelation. Many calls it the only Prophetical book. Actually, all the Bible is prophetical, in the sense that the Word of God leads us to God and to be reunited to Him.

If we consider the book of Revelation or Apocalypses as a book that tells us about the future, or, equivalently, if we consider its prophetical aspect as being capable of telling us the future, and the future being future historical events, we are misled on both accounts: a- describing the book b- understanding the deep meaning of being prophetical according to the final revelation the Lord is bringing us.

In fact, after the Revelation that the Lord came to offer us, we do not expect any other revelation. The newness in fact, according to Christianity, consists in diving repeatedly deeper in Christ who is God and discovering always new things in Him. He is the same, but since he is God, we have all eternity to discover him and be in awe, minute after minute, for all eternity. The

---

[9] See how *Evagrius Ponticus* understood Theology: being in the Son, contemplating the Father in the Holy Spirit.

wonders of his being are endless. In him consists all newness. He is the Day that never dawns, and he is present to us (by the way this is the meaning of Sunday. We are called to live every week as an ascent in circles that go always deeper, toward the Divinity of the Risen Lord).

The book of Revelation is the book that holds a series of visions given to John to help the Church who was going through great difficulties, to help her understand the true meaning of what was happening in order not to go astray or be disheartened by the exterior tough events of trials, persecutions and darkness.

This book is the most focused book on the essential core of Theology: it shows the goal, it doesn't lose time in exterior events or tales, it stays focused on the spiritual warfare in order to reach the Goal. We will see in this article – God willing – at least in what consists the goal.

Let us first notice something unique in the Church, the liturgical placement of the book of Revelation. In the Roman Latin tradition, the book is read alternately with the book of Daniel in the last week of the Liturgical year. This shows that the book is telling us the final goal, what we are aiming for. It dispossesses us from all that is futile and keeps us focused on the essential message of the Lord. Truly it still continues to look mysterious, but its liturgical placement is indicative of what it is. In the Coptic liturgy, the whole book is read and celebrated liturgically during the night of Good Friday, in fact in the early hours of Holy Saturday. It is celebrated with various hymns, taken from the book of Revelation, incense, Candelabre (lampstand) in the middle of the church and anointing in the end of the liturgy of the whole assembly (please see at the end of this article more details). Why reading the entire book of Revelation while the Lord is dead? In fact, it is exactly timed in the Holy Week between Jesus' death and his resurrection. It is true that at this moment we believe that He goes to all the dead, to announce to them his Redemption, to offer it and free all who died in Hope of His Redemption. In a sense, Redemption starts to be applied, given. Freedom from Hades is operated. For us, who are on earth, this time is the time of huge paradox! It is the time of total absence of the Lord and it is the time of maximum hope where we search for Our Lady, the only one who during these dark hours of death stood fast and believed in the Words of her son and Lord: "I will rise again in the Third day". It is the time of total loss, like the apostles, we feel that the earth lost her Redeemer, we do struggle with our weak faith. It is a dark moment. If you happen to enter in a Roman Latin Catholic church after the liturgy of Good Friday at 3 pm, you will notice how the church is empty. The altar is naked, the Tabernacle is opened and empty, no images, no statues are visible… total emptiness. The darkness in its true meaning.

The book of Revelation helps us go through the most difficult times and come out of it as winners. Let us see what is at stake.

The book starts with a first and fundamental vision, the vision of the victorious Lord. This vision is of total importance because the whole book is based on it. It is a vision of Christ and the vision takes time to describe different aspects of the risen and victorious Lord. These aspects are of utmost importance. Why? Because they are given to us, but not yet. They are the object of our dearest hope. They are the object of the promise of the Lord: we are about to undergo the greatest battle in our life, and the Lord says to us that if we win, we will get Him.

The battle, struggles and trials are composed of seven steps. As if in us, we need to grow seven steps, win seven times in order to get the whole Christ, the Whole Vision. This is why the entire book is set to lead us to a Wedding, the Wedding between Him and each one of us, all of us constituting the Bride of the Lamb, his bride (see chapters 21 and 22 describing the bride and the wedding).

Note: the Gospel of St. John is in fact the rendering of the book of his Revelations in a more approachable way, and you can easily notice that the first step/sign in the Gospel the one that give the entire architecture of his Gospel is the Signe of the Wedding in Cana!!

Here is the account of the fundamental vision, the description of Christ who is the **Tree of Life**, the Groom, our recompense. By the end of the book, after having gone through all the trials and coming out of them victorious, our recompense is Him. This vision describes in fact the one who is our recompense, he is ours in the end.

"I John, your brother and fellow-partaker in the tribulation and kingdom and perseverance in Jesus, was in the island called Patmos on account of the word of God and the testimony of Jesus. 10 I was in the Spirit on the Lord's day, and I heard behind me a loud voice, like that of a trumpet, 11 saying, "What you see, write in a book and send to the seven churches: to Ephesus, and to Smyrna, and to Pergamum, and to Thyatira, and to Sardis, and to Philadelphia, and to Laodicea."

12 And I turned to see the voice that was speaking with me. And having turned, I saw seven golden lampstands, 13 and in the midst of the lampstands, One like the Son of Man, having been clothed to the feet, and having been girded about at the breasts with a golden sash. 14 Now His head and His hairs are white like wool, white as snow; and His eyes are like a flame of fire; 15 and His feet are like fine bronze, as having been refined in a furnace; and His voice is like the voice of many waters; 16 and He is holding in His right hand seven stars, and a sharp two-edged sword is going forth out of His mouth; and His face is like the sun shining in its full strength. 17 And when I saw Him, I fell at His feet as though dead. And He placed His right hand upon me, saying, "Fear not. I am the First and the Last, 18and the Living One. And I was dead, and behold I am living to the ages of the ages, and I have the keys of Death and of Hades.

19 Therefore write the things that you have seen, and the things that are, and the things that are about to take place after these, 20 the mystery of the seven stars, which you saw on My right hand, and the seven golden lampstands: The seven stars are the angels of the seven churches, and the seven lampstands are the seven churches." (Rev 1:1-19)

I preferred to put the entire 19 verses in order to show not only the vision in itself (vv. 12-16) but also its context, the verses before and after help us understand better the centrality of the vision, to whom it is given (the seven churches), the angels of the seven churches (their leaders),… It deserves a long explanation, but let us focus on this article's subject: The Goal, the recompense the Lord wants to give us.

Right after this vision, we have seven messages sent to "seven churches" and in each of these messages we find the same structure. Here is the first one and let us see the structure:

*"1 To the messenger of the church in Ephesus write: These things says the One holding the seven stars in His right hand, walking in the midst of the seven golden lampstands. 2 I know your works and your labour and endurance, and that you are not able to tolerate evil ones. And you have tested those claiming to be apostles and are not, and you have found them false. 3 And you have perseverance, and have endured for the sake of My name, and have not grown weary. 4 But I have against you that you have abandoned your first love. 5Remember therefore from where you have fallen, and repent, and do the first works. But if not, I am coming to you, and I will remove your lampstand out of its place, unless you should repent. 6 But you have this, that you hate the works of the Nicolaitans, which I also hate. 7 The one having an ear, let him hear what the Spirit says to the churches. To the one overcoming, I will give to him to eat of the **Tree of Life**, which is in the paradise of God."* (Gn 2:1-7)

First, we have the description of one aspect of the Lord, taken in fact from the initial vision (please see and compare)! Here we have: *"says the One holding the seven stars in His right hand, walking in the midst of the seven golden lampstands"*. The text suggests that in addition to identifying the sender of the message, we also acquire knowledge about a particular aspect of the sender that is closely connected to the reward or compensation.

We have first a praise, source of encouragement:

"2 I know your works and your labour and endurance, and that you are not able to tolerate evil ones. And you have tested those claiming to be apostles and are not, and you have found them false. 3 And you have perseverance, and have endured for the sake of My name, and have not grown weary."

The Lord doesn't start with a blame. He points out to the good things already achieved. And from that praise he draws strength for the hearer in order to set the challenge, the effort to produce: in fact, thereafter comes a blame, or reproach given by the Lord. It underlines a weakness. Think of our seven mortal sins, who are like seven potentialities in us, they can offer either grave sins, or glorious virtues and therefore recompenses. These potentialities are the "churches" to whom the seven messages are sent. Do you remember the seven mortal sins? Think of the them as a great source of information: we

45

have seven areas in our being, and they are capable of the worst but they are also capable of the best. In our case, the Lord, described in one of the seven characteristics shown in the main vision, tells us that he is our glorious recompense, in one of the seven greats aspects of his total being.

Notice he says: "to the messenger" or "angel" of the Church of… he is the head of this church. "mortal sins" are also named "capital sins" because they are heads (capita in Latin) of many other sins of their type. Here is the blame directed to this potentiality, the Ephesus church:

4 But I have against you that you have abandoned your first love. 5 Remember therefore from where you have fallen, and repent, and do the first works. But if not, I am coming to you, and I will remove your lampstand out of its place, unless you should repent.
Taken aback, one can lose faith again. This is why the Lord send another encouragement: *6But you have this, that you hate the works of the Nicolaitans, which I also hate.*
Now we have the end of the message, which goes this way: *7 The one having an ear, let him hear what the Spirit says to the churches. To the one overcoming, I will give to him to eat of the **Tree of Life**, which is in the paradise of God."*

The Lord wants each one of us to identify in our life what these messages alludes to and get from him courage and undergo the challenge and win. In order to give us more courage and strength he gives us a promise of recompense, and here it is: *To the one overcoming, I will give to him to eat of the **Tree of Life**, which is in the Paradise of God."*

He is bringing us to the beginnings: *"Out of the ground the LORD God gave growth to every tree that is pleasing to the eye and good for food. And in the middle of the garden were the **Tree of Life** and the tree of the knowledge of good and evil."* (Genesis 2:9) and after the fall, after the original sin: *"Then the LORD God said, "Behold, the man has become like one of Us, knowing good and evil. And now, lest he reach out his hand and take also from the **Tree of Life**, and eat, and live forever…""* (Genesis 3:22)

The **Tree of Life** is the Lord himself! we often forget that in Paradise we had two trees and not only one. We focus a lot on the tree that is the source of all our troubles, the tree of the knowledge of good and evil, the tree that will be used by the devil to tempt us: *"For God knows that when you eat from it your eyes will be opened, and you will be like God, **knowing good and evil.**"* (Genesis 3:5) Like eve we think that there is only one tree in the middle of the Garden and that it is this one. In fact there is another tree and we were allowed to eat from it, it is the main tree: the **Tree of Life**!! We forgot it. We overlooked it and were attracted by another tree, close by, the tree of knowing good and evil.

As a consequence of this sin, we are deprived from the main tree, the **Tree of Life**.
Amazingly, undergoing the trials, growing spiritually, and winning, we are admitted to eat back again from this Tree at the centre of the Garden: the **Tree of Life**! *"To the one overcoming, I will give to him to eat of the **Tree of Life**, which is in the Paradise of God."* This **Tree of Life** is the Risen Lord himself (see the icon above).

When we ask ourselves: "what is the goal of our life here on earth?" we should remember that if we undergo the good fight and the real warfare, there are promises to obtain. This is only the first one, let us see the sum of the six remaining ones, because they are for us:

2- *"The one overcoming shall not be injured by the second death."* (Rev 2:11)

3- *"The one overcoming, I will give to him the manna having been hidden, and I will give to him a white stone, and on the stone new a name having been written, which no one has known, except the one receiving it."* (Rev 2:17)

4- *"And the one overcoming and keeping My works until the end, I will give to him authority over the nations, 27and he will shepherd them with a rod of iron, as the vessels of the potter are broken in pieces—just as I also have received from My Father. 28And I will give to him the morning star."* (Rev 2:26-28)

5- *"The one overcoming thus will be clothed in white garments. And I will never blot out his name from the book of life, and I will confess his name before My Father and before His angels."* (Rev 3:5)

6- *"The one overcoming, I will make him a pillar in the temple of My God, and he shall not go out anymore. And I will write upon him the name of My God, and the name of the city of My God, the new Jerusalem coming down out of heaven from My God, and My new name."* (Rev 3:12)

7- *"The one overcoming, I will give to him to sit with Me on My throne, as I also overcame and sat down with My Father on His throne."* (Rev 3:21)

In the darkness of this life here on earth, we are offered the sum of these 7 promises. These are the Lamps that guide us, that attract us and constitute our Christian Hope. To add something more to this prophecy in any teaching is dangerous: *"I testify to everyone hearing the words of the prophecy of this book: If anyone should add to these things, God will add unto him the plagues having been written in this book. 19 And if anyone should take away from the words of the book of this prophecy, **God will take away his part from the Tree of Life**, and out of the holy city, of those having been written in this book."* (Rev 22:18-19)

Surprisingly, what is offered as a recompense (having part back again to the **Tree of Life**, the one we were deprived of) is taken again. These verses of Rev 22:18-19 are as sharp and menacing as the one given to Adam and Eve in the beginning: *"And the LORD God commanded him, "You may eat freely from every tree of the garden, 17but you must not eat from the tree of the knowledge of good and evil; for in the day that you eat of it, you will surely die.""* (Rev 2:16-17) Adding anything to the words of this prophecy, i.e. offering any other object of Hope to any human being, is acting as a false prophet in the name of the Lord, and this incurs "death", which means not being able to eat from the "**Tree of Life**" for ever. The warning is very powerful. Theology should abide with what God says, and only with what God says and Promises.

In these difficult moments the Church is undergoing today, and it is very much possible to have even darker moments in the near future, we need to focus on the essential message of the Lord, the core of it and not to be distracted by anything else, and mainly to nourish ourselves with the real object of Hope: his Promises.

Let us together, sum up the seven promises for the winners and meditate them in order to fill our heart with courage, such courage to go through the trials by the grace of God and come out of them victorious, winners in Him. He is our recompense. The first Vision that St. John has is a vision of Christ and Christ is our only Hope. Let us focus on Christ and on the infinite beauty of his being, let us meditate the Prophecy of St. John, let us draw close to The Theologian. Amen.

Note: The *Night of Apocalypse* in the Coptic Church

"The night of Great Friday [Good Friday] is called the *Night of Apocalypse* because it is on this night that we read the entire Holy Book of Revelation. On this night we celebrate the descent of Our Lord and Saviour Jesus Christ into the pit of Hades to restore all those who died on the hope of the resurrection to Paradise. The church gathers around the tomb of the Lord Jesus Christ the whole night in prayers and rituals. This special night is begun with the opening of the altar curtain, which symbolizes when Our Lord and Savior Jesus Christ opened the gates of Paradise on the great Friday. The Night of Apocalypse is divided into eight major parts: Midnight Praises, Prayer of Prime Hour, Morning Raising of Incense, Prayers of the Third and Sixth Hours, Revelation, Prayers of the Ninth Hour, the Divine Liturgy, and the Prayers of the Eleventh Hour."

"After the Third and Sixth Hours Prayers have been read, the church begins to read the Holy Book of Revelation. The Holy Book of Revelation is read on Night of the Apocalypse because the Holy Book of Revelation refers to the bride of the Lord Jesus Christ; the Church. In the Holy Gospel of St. John, St. John calls Our Lord and Saviour Jesus Christ the "bridegroom" (John 3:29) and in the Holy Book of Revelation 21:9 St. John refers to the "bride" of the Lord Jesus Christ; the church…and tells St. John…"Come I will show you the bride, the Lamb's wife." Our Lord and Saviour Jesus Christ shed His blood on the cross and descended into Hades to get his bride, the saints and then opened the gates of Paradise. Now there is a bridegroom and we await the bride by reading the description of the church in the Holy Book of Revelation.

The story of salvation is that God the Father chose a bride for His Son, who paid for His bride, not with gold or silver, but with His Precious Blood. We are engaged to the Lord Jesus Christ; purified by His water and blood (Ephesians 5:25), wedded at the moment of His death on Great Friday.

All the hymns of the holy book of revelations are related to the bride of Christ: the church. These hymns call the bride to listen to the voice of the Holy Spirit, enumerate the number the sealed bride, the song of the bride (Alleluia), and the foundation of the heavenly Jerusalem (the bride of Christ).

The book of revelation is read between the Sixth and the Ninth hour since at that time the Lord Jesus Christ was crucified, shed His blood and descended into Hades to restore Adam and his children to the paradise of joy.

The anointing of oil by the priests to the congregation before the Divine Liturgy is referred to in the Holy Book of Revelation 7:2-8, in which the servants of God must have sealed upon their foreheads. We are anointed with oil to seal us; to say that we are the bride of the Lord Jesus Christ. Following this, the Ninth Hour is prayed in preparation for the Divine Liturgy." (H.G. Bishop Youssef, *Bishop of the Coptic Orthodox Diocese of the Southern United States*)

What Is Holiness?

To understand "holiness" a number of facts need to be underlined.

First, holiness is a fundamental issue in our life. Secondly, understanding the nature of holiness is therefore fundamental.

Two further significant facts to look at are: first, since the early sixties, with Council Vatican II, we have been reminded that Jesus calls all of us to Holiness (see: *Lumen Gentium*, Chapter 5, The Universal Call to Holiness). And this is very positive.

Secondly, details about what holiness is and how to attain it remain until today difficult to access. Therefore these concepts remain very imprecise and vague. We often respond with general ideas and directions, but when it comes to details, we lack a great deal of practical insight.

Some people think that by just abiding by Christian Dogma, Liturgy (+ Sacraments) and Morality it is enough [or worse: it guarantees you] to reach holiness. Our popular understanding of "holiness" is one thing, but to be more precise is something totally different.

It is important to notice that our understanding of: **1- The Cross** (what Jesus accomplishes on the Cross), **2- Easter**, **3- Baptism** and 4- **Christian life** are directly related. Also that, in the end, all will obviously bring us to holiness. Our understanding of these four realities has shrunk significantly from the original view/understanding – with dramatic consequences on our understanding of holiness. It has shrunk to a frightening point. To explain it, I'll take an example: the Promise given to Abraham to give him the Land.
After 430 years of "slavery" in Egypt, God decided that the time was right to act and save His People. We all have a geographical idea of the journey of the people of God, from Egypt to the Promised Land (see the map).

This Journey was made in 40 years. (Remember that this journey wouldn't take more than 3 days walking, if you take a more direct route) I would divide this journey into 4 parts (not like the map shows). This is my choice, just to make my point.

51

1- One night: walking to the Red Sea and crossing it (admittedly, you may add a few days or weeks while Moses and the Pharaoh are defying each other, with the consequent plagues of Egypt following).

2- Two years: from the crossing until the area called Kadesh Barnea is reached.

3- Thirty eight years: going in circles around the area of Kadesh.

4- Finally entering the Promised Land: crossing the Jordan, fighting against the local population (7 tribes).

The full journey comprises numbers 1 + 2 + 3 + 4.

I am using the full journey as an example of our spiritual Christian Journey, heading toward Holiness (the "Promised Land"). The whole action that Jesus accomplishes on **the Cross** comprises in itself the full journey. Saving us is not just taking us from Egypt to the desert (crossing the Red Sea)!! It is the same with **Baptism**: being baptised is not just crossing the Red Sea, finishing with the slavery of the Devil (Pharaoh) like the Fathers of the Church used to say. The full realisation of Baptism is to reach the Promised land. Wouldn't you agree?

The same goes for **Easter**: during the Easter Vigil we focus a lot on the essential reading of the crossing of the Red Sea. Nothing wrong with that. But crossing the desert, spending 40 years in it, crossing the River Jordan, have no impact on our understanding of Easter. We often, traditionally use the Easter Vigil to Baptise catechumens. Does it encourage us more toward this "reduction"/this poverty in our understanding of the concepts as illustrated above? Well, the debate is open.

The same thing is true of our **Christian daily life**: we measure everything by one measure: "am I in the state of grace or not? If not, I do have to go to confession. So my life becomes a question of being or not being in a "state of grace". It is like saying: "did I cross the desert or not?". Ok, fair enough. But where is the Desert in our Christian life? Do we see it? Do we understand its deep meaning? Do we understand manna? Receiving the Law? Not listening to God, and having to go in circles for 38 years until we are totally purified (see Numbers, Chapter 16)? Having to cross the waters of the river Jordan? Having to go and fight 7 tribes?

It seems that everything depends on: "am I in the state of grace or not?", and the rest will take care of itself. I just need to pray, to go to Mass, to confess, to perform good deeds, and holiness will come by itself. So: "take it easy, sit down and relax. Take a deep breath, you are saved from the Red Sea. The rest will come, you just need to be a good Christian."

Crossing the Red Sea is fundamentally like seeing Saul being knocked off his horse and falling, blind, under the powerful liberating light of Jesus.

All that comes afterwards, however, is infinitely much more: it is when Paul takes time to grow (he spends 3 years in Arabia)… and then works, serves… Saint Paul's life doesn't revolve around his falling from his horse. Ironically it seems that for us, holiness is about falling from our horse.

"Falling from our horse" is technically called: "conversion". But then, our Christian life, Baptism, the Cross, Easter, are simply reduced to a BINARY level: I am or not in the state of grace (1,0). And, if I am not, I should go to confession. All the rest will be – roughly – fine. (Yes "roughly", as you will notice.) This is what some will later call: holiness.

People think, vaguely, that Holiness will/might come, roughly, automatically, by itself, as if by magic.

I am not sure of that at all. I wouldn't plan my entire life around "roughly" and "maybe".

A friend just posed this question: *"The Catholic Church I think defines a saint as somebody who has **practised heroic virtue**. So we can talk about holiness as **heroic virtue**. <u>Benedict XIV</u>, an 18th century pope, stated: "In order to be **heroic**, a Christian virtue must enable its owner to perform virtuous actions with uncommon promptitude, ease, and pleasure, from supernatural motives and without human reasoning, with self-abnegation and full control over his natural inclinations."*

And most people would say that one needs to pray for the Holy Spirit to achieve a life of heroic virtue.

What are your thoughts on this definition of holiness and the possibility of achieving it?"

The first stage of my reply to this question is as follows:

First, I would like to confirm that what the question posed is correct and is still valid today. Indeed, we have this following paragraph in the Catechism of the Catholic Church: *"828 By canonising some of the faithful, i.e., by solemnly proclaiming that they **practised heroic virtue** and lived in fidelity to God's grace, the Church recognises the power of the Spirit of holiness within her and sustains the hope of believers by proposing the saints to them as models and intercessors."*[10]

Before moving on to give my thoughts on this issue, I would like to come back to the words that were used in the question and make a clarification. This "old" way of defining Holiness, of trying to "see" it in somebody, is still used today. This is how we find out if somebody is a saint or not. We go through the virtues, and question witnesses of his life who would support the fact that he practised them in a heroic way. We are not God, we cannot see into the soul and spirit of a potential saint, so we simply do the sort of

---

[10] See on the Vatican website the Apostolic Constitution : "Divinus Perfectionis Magister".

work a "Spiritual Director" would do, but more in the form of a trial (ecclesiastical tribunal).

The question focused on the adjective "heroic": this is very good; it is a fair definition (phenomenological, i.e. describing it from outside, from what is seen). I would now like to focus on "virtue". A saint is not invited to practise any virtue, but specific virtues: Faith, Hope, Love/Charity, Justice, Prudence, Fortitude, Temperance,…

Temperance   Prudence   Fortitude   Justice

Virtues are like formed muscles (remember the bodybuilders). In order to grow they need:

1- muscles (i.e. the faculties of the soul: mind, will,..),

2- nutrients (from the blood, that nourish the muscles): the Grace of God

3- exercise (the specific acts of each virtue to be repeated).

The whole structure of the virtues is like, if you will, the muscles on the skeleton.

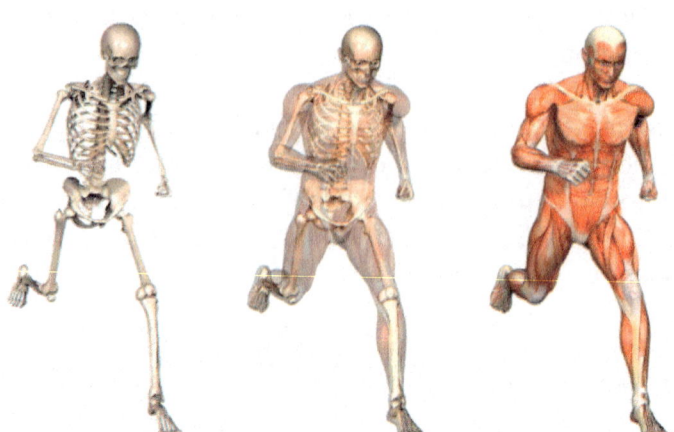

So, when the Church wants to know if somebody has become holy (obviously after his/her death), the "tribunal" acts like a doctor of the soul and of the spirit and tries to perform a "scan" of the "muscles" (i.e. virtues) and to determine their state. But, ultimately, since we are not God and we can't be 100% sure of something "invisible" to the naked eye and subject to such variations (the human soul), the Church considers the necessity of a Miracle, in order to be sure of God's judgement.

Now, of course, we need to learn what the virtues are and learn how to make them grow until they reach the "heroic state".

This analysis also reflects the state of spiritual theology of that time. Nothing wrong with it, on the contrary. Aristotle, Saint Thomas Aquinas, and even up to Garrigou-Lagrange (1877-1964).

Now the question is: how can we make all these muscles work? Workout, workout, workout… How can we do it "out of Love for Jesus", not "out of the need for a 'workout' "?
I am old enough to say that I knew of books for novices (first year of religious life) where they had to pick a virtue per week or per month and work on it. In the book there were lists of the virtues, with different examples and applications. Fair enough.

But we all know that in order to reach that "perfection" of virtue described by Pope Benedict XIV (see the description given in the question) we need to go through **a journey of purification** as well, and enter into deeper states of contemplation and receive abundant graces.

In order to know the journey well, you have the book with the **11 diagrams** commented: "The Spiritual Journey, The Setting for Christian Hope" (see in Amazon).

The journey itself of the formation of a virtue **has various layers** – still according to Saint Thomas Aquinas:

The first layer comes from our education: the natural exercise of various virtues (justice, prudence, fortitude, temperance, studiositas, magnanimity,…). Aristotle is a good master here. He was adopted by Saint Thomas Aquinas, of course, putting his teaching into a Christian framework.

A second layer would add the supernatural intervention of the Grace of God, like new "blood" injected into the "muscle" (that will produce the christian virtue). This is fundamental and helps us understand the big difference between a virtue practised by a Greek philosopher for instance, and the virtue practised by a Christian person, even the humblest one. The Holy Spirit enters in us and starts to make deep changes and elevates our exercise of the virtue (the muscle) to a higher level. Remember that **The Goal** is high – God – and that **The Means** is high – God Himself – as well as the Holy Spirit.

A third layer: when the second level has been exercised for a long time, with perseverance, faithfulness, the Action of the Holy Spirit increases and goes deeper, really transforming the "muscles" (the habits) in God, in Jesus, making the "movement" (the acts) much easier, more fluid, more spontaneous (see the description quoted, from Benedict XIVth). The result of this transformation is that the Gifts of the Holy Spirit (the 7 gifts) intervene and act in a smooth way. **The sails** (7 Gifts) are high up, so when the Wind blows (the Holy Spirit) it is capable of moving the boat (the soul): Saint Paul, in his letters, invites his fellow Christians to be guided/moved by the Holy Spirit.

Nobody can challenge this "anatomy of Holiness".

But the questions remains: is this "system" possible? Or is it just the anatomy of a beautiful wishful thought?

How can we reach these stages? What are the means?

Are we just supposed – like athletes – to repeat acts, specific acts in order to encourage through them growth, a habit, a "muscle": a Virtue? To a degree, it looks too cold as a "system" or as a recipe for "holiness", too mechanical, too artificial. This is exactly where we are today: in a state of stasis since the 1950s…

This is why, offering any Christian as a central task, the duty to eat, digest and assimilated the "Bread" God gives us in each Mass, is for me the most powerful way to reach holiness. The Bread is: **1- His Word** and **2- His Body and Blood**. In order to digest this "Daily Bread" we need today to pay great attention to the extension of this *manducation* (act of eating) that makes today's bread more efficient and long-lasting. The two operations ('ways of prayer' if you will) that help us digest the Bread received during the daily Mass are: **1- Practising 'Lectio Divina' 2- Practising the 'Prayer of the Heart'**.

We need to have a **personal relationship with Jesus**, with the help of the Holy Spirit. Jesus and His Holy Spirit are our main Masters. They are our Holiness. We need to grow in Them; we need Them to grow in us.

"Imagination" and "Faculties"

In our journey toward holiness there are pitfalls and the need for discernment. Of prime importance are two aspects, voiced by Saint Teresa of Avila in the following paragraph where she mentions the difference between the "faculties" and the "imagination". What does she mean by this? And how can learning the difference affect our understanding of real holiness?

"I like the way in which some souls, when they are at prayer, think that, for God's sake, they would be glad if they could be humbled and put to open

shame – and then try to conceal quite a slight failure. Oh, and if they should be accused of anything that they have not done – ! God save us from having to listen to them then! Let anyone who cannot bear trials like that be very careful to pay no heed to the resolutions he may have made when he was alone. For they could not in fact have been resolutions made by the will (a genuine act of the will is quite another matter); they must have been due to some freak of the imagination. The devil makes good use of the imagination in practising his surprises and deceptions, and there are many such which he can practise on women, or on unlettered persons, because we do not understand **the difference between the faculties** *and* **the imagination**, *and thousands of other things belonging to the interior life. Oh, sisters, how clearly it can be seen what love of your neighbour really means to some of you, and what an imperfect stage it has reached in others! If you understood the importance of this virtue to us all you would strive after nothing but gaining it."* (*Interior Castle*, V,III,10)

This passage is taken from Saint Theresa's book "The Interior Castle", Fifth Mansions, Chapter III, paragraph 10. This chapter is of great importance because it addresses the pitfalls of "illusion" and "spiritual pride" in spiritual life, and in our journey toward holiness.

In spiritual life, when striving toward holiness, what is important for us to achieve is a good healthy **will**, i.e. a healthy virtue. "Virtue" is a "good habit". A "habit" comes from the "repetition of good acts" (i.e. loving your neighbour). Having a Spiritual Life means that on a daily basis one practises – amongst other things – hours of "Prayer of the Heart". However, if the Prayer of the Heart is not accompanied by "Lectio Divina" (i.e. putting into practise with our will the **will** of God), we end up entering into deeper and deeper illusions: thinking that we are growing, thinking that by the fact of practising the "prayer of the heart" we are close to God, we are spiritually fine, we are saints.

"thinking that" means deceiving myself, **imagining** something that doesn't exist. One can lie to oneself to the point of starting to believe one's own lies. In order to do that one uses the **imagination**. Today, we can easily, therefore, consider imagination as a "faculty" of the soul.

The most important **faculties** of the soul, at least for Theresa of Avila are: **Mind**, **Will** and **Memory**. She and Saint John of the Cross separate themselves here from the thinking of St Augustine, for he uses only the **Mind** and the **Will**. These are called "rational faculties", i.e. the faculties of the rational soul (opposed to the animal soul), the higher part of the soul. Listening to God in order to discover His Will for us, and putting, through our will, His Word and His Will into practise is a **key issue** in spiritual life. This is why I always stress the fact that we have always to practise "Lectio Divina" and "Prayer of the Heart" together, (but obviously not in the same hour), for they are the two "legs" we use in order to "walk". As you can see, the mechanism of the Prayer of the Heart is the Action of God in a supra-conscious area in us: the spirit. We can't see the roots of our being (i.e. the spirit). They are real, but hidden like the roots of a tree. During the Prayer of the Heart we are not supposed to see or to feel anything ("seeing" and "feeling" happen in the conscious part), because the Action of God is happening deep in us. And even if we feel or see something (in the conscious part), we don't have to pay attention to it. We need to remain in the general attitude of love, having our heart/spirit immersed in Jesus. This means that our mind and our imagination are left alone, free, and potential victims of the illusions of the devil. Since we are practising the Prayer of the Heart, the Devil can try to convince us that we have reached the heights of holiness. He can then divert our attention from Lectio Divina (thus creating a weakness in our faculties: mind and will). So the time spent in "Prayer of the Heart" can make us the prey of the Devil.

Obviously, Saint Theresa doesn't use the expression "lectio divina", but in the end of the day she gives us its real content, the core of what is needed: we need to love our neighbour and if we don't do so, we shouldn't deceive ourselves, thinking that we have reached the goal of spiritual life. Saint John in his first letter gives us the same warning: how can you pretend to love God whom you don't see (or feel) (Prayer of the Heart) and not to love your neighbour that you see?! (see 1John..,..) There is a big difference between illusion (just the work of imagination) and a human mind and a human will that listen to the Will of God and put it into practice.

On top of that, and Saint Teresa says it in this beautiful Chapter III: if we do love our neighbour, the love that God pours into us during the Prayer of the Heart will increase significantly. Saint John of the Cross will mention this Golden Rule as well in his Spiritual Canticle (See *Spiritual Canticle*, A, 12,11; *Living Flame of Love*, I,6,34).

In another place, too, she says: if you practise the Prayer of the Heart and don't work on growing in virtue (activating the mind and the will, according to the Will of God) you'll remain like dwarfs (spiritual dwarfs, i.e. very weak).

One of the tactics the Devil uses with spiritual persons is to convince them (to deceive them) that they have reached the Goal (union with God or so), and by doing that, **they stop making their efforts to grow, of real growth**, especially in loving their neighbour – the result is to go backward. Living in illusion is a very good tactic of the devil for more spiritual persons. This is why, from the first lines of the Fifth Mansions, Saint Theresa of Avila mentions the spiritual illusion: "the Devil appearing like an Angel of light" (quote from Saint Paul). Obviously the Devil changes his tactics and adapts them to the spiritual level of the person. He won't tempt the spiritual person with something clearly evil. On the contrary, now that the person is determined to reach God, the Devil will tempt her with "the appearance of Good". A fake "good thing": he tries to convince the person that he/she is with God, that he/she reached Him… "hooray, now rest and enjoy". He has then won.

Theresa of Avila, as a real Master of Spiritual life, has to warn us about this temptation. And in order to discover it, one of the most important elements of discernment is to be able to distinguish between **an act of will** from anything else like: feelings, emotions, imagination… i.e. illusions. While an act of the will is real, free, voluntary, any feeling, emotion, imagination is more of a passive, receptive state that doesn't necessarily involve any change in us, any use of our will.

Therefore, discernment and discipleship (through Spiritual Direction) are vital at certain stages. Seeking Advice/Discernment is an implicit act of proclamation of the Incarnation: God is present amongst us and wants/loves to speak to us through our Spiritual Director (but watch out, we need to choose the right one, because the "spiritual son" will be like the "spiritual father" says the Catechism, quoting Saint John of the Cross. There is no magic here.). See Ascent of Mount Carmel Book 2 Chapter 22, second part.

Important Remark: As we can see here, imagination (which is considered as a faculty), can be the easy prey of the Devil. Of course, what Saint Theresa of Avila means by "imagination" could be explained as well as an act of the mind (producing thoughts) with no practical application (no implications for the will). Like the one who reads, reads and reads spiritual books and ends up by believing that he reached the state he is reading about. Reading can have a "hypnotic" effect on him (with the help of the Devil). But, but: there is a difference between this illusion and convincing ourselves, strengthening our desire and willingness to serve God, setting high goals, and motivating ourselves with great thoughts. Indeed, in her writings, Saint Theresa invites us, on the contrary, to motivate ourselves by setting high goals and widening the horizon of our mind. Something will come out of "many good desires", while nothing will come out from not harbouring "high goals" and "good desires". In fact, Saint Theresa of Avila is very modern: nowadays we do hear a lot about the role of visualisation in order to achieve high, complicated goals/acts. First you run it through your mind: you visualise it. The brain (neurological pathways) is then activated accordingly and creates new pathways and, by repeating the visualisation, you strengthen these new pathways, and you will be able to put what you visualised into practice. This is not "illusion" or ill imagination, or deceiving ourselves. On the contrary, this is opening the way for the mind and will in order to achieve new directions given by God. Saint Theresa of Avila is not jeopardising imagination and creativity – on the contrary, she is warning us of a false "imagination" that doesn't lead anywhere.

Here, "imagination" and "mind" are very close. You can almost repeat what Saint Theresa said in this way: *"because we do not understand* **the difference between the mind and the will**…*"* i.e. we don't see that **thinking** about something is not yet **doing** it. Saint Paul says it bluntly: the good I want to achieve (what my mind sees and knows as "good") my will doesn't put it into practise! My will is still ill, not transformed into the will of God. Mind and will are divided.

In other words, it connects up with what Saint James says in his letter: faith is not enough! Believing is good, it opens us up and connects us with God in order to receive His Holy Spirit. But a faith that doesn't have real applications, that doesn't spring into real practical acts, remains an illusion. In other words: you may have the Holy Spirit at the reach of your hands, but if you don't put into practise His Will, then He remains at your door and never really enters. You are deceiving yourself greatly.

Focusing On Holiness

The question concerning how to focus on holiness is a fundamental one to ask ourselves because, according to the Gospel and to the ordinary teaching of the Church, we are all called to become saints. Therefore it is of vital importance to define: « What constitutes a Saint ? » or « What is Holiness? » and, as a consequence, another question arises : « How does one become a Saint ? »

What is Holiness?

Going beyond general definitions, seeking to get closer to a description of its very essence, here are some definitions of Holiness that you might agree with: to be like God. To be totally transformed in God. To be fully united to God. To be one with God. To recapture the "image and likeness" of God that we have lost. To realise to the full the Seed of our Baptism. To have Jesus in us, fully living and acting. To reach the fullness of the Height of Jesus. To reach the fullness of Charity.

It is true that Baptism makes us Holy, it is true that Christians were called by St Paul "the Saints". But in truth, all the above definitions or descriptions, if taken with a true examination of conscience, lead us to this implicit truth: Holiness is a goal, we are not totally there yet, we are on a continuous journey of spiritual growth.

The Journey toward Holiness

The notion of growth implies the existence of a process of transformation, sanctification, purification, divinisation. This process could be simply seen as a Journey. Jesus himself presents himself to us as the Way ("I am the Way" (John 14:6)), the Way to intimacy with the Father, to Union with the Father.

Having to undergo a "spiritual journey" means that we need to go through different stages. The notion of "stages of growth" is directly linked to the notion of the "journey of growth".

Spiritual Doctrine of the Church

Now a question arises: do we have any teaching on these two subjects: 1-the Goal, 2- the stages of growth to achieve this Goal? Yes, we have: "The Spiritual Doctrine deposited by God in the Church". This Spiritual Doctrine proceeds from the Gospel, develops throughout the ages and leads us back to the Gospel with a deeper understanding of it. According to "the Spiritual Doctrine of the Church", we have a description of Holiness and indirectly it comes with the exposition of "The Stages of the Journey" that leads to Holiness.

Toward a Definition of Holiness

Holiness is seen as the completion of the meaning of Baptism, of being immersed to the full in the Divine Life of the Trinity and its operations. St John of the Cross, in his book "the Living Flame of Love", describes Christian Death, as one more act of Love where the Holy Spirit extracts the soul-spirit from the body (i.e. the mortal life), like a Precious Stone or Pearl from its case, making it dive finally, freely and totally into God's being. In defining Christian death, St John of the Cross is in fact also helping us to understand the concept of holiness. Holiness is the completion of the full journey of Growth, by reaching the fullness of Love: dying in Christ, is a final extra act of Love, moved by the Holy Spirit, toward our deepest Centre: God.

In doing so, St John of the Cross is giving us a new meaning for human life and time. Between the lines he is saying to us: the unit of counting "time" could be just the ticking of a clock, i.e. our bodily growth and aging, or, it could coincide, if lived on a daily basis in fullness by fulfilling every day's measure of Growth, with the unit of our transformation.

Time Changes

Jesus teaches us that every day brings its own effort and therefore measure of Growth. Every day is then an opportunity for growth, a series of Providential events that will challenge us, in a neat and positive way, to become opportunities for Growth, helping us to progress step by step toward the fullness of God.

There is a possibility then to "waste time" or to "gain time". I waste time when the door opens for an opportunity to be taken, for a challenge to be undergone and for transformation to result, by the Grace of God, and I don't take it! Time is used well, to the fullness of its unit or measure (the day), when I am lead by the Grace of God, do God's Will, and take with His Help one extra step of Growth and transformation in Him.

The result is: Holiness and a Life of Holiness (i.e. a life that leads to holiness).

Time (i.e. life) could be used well, and be considered "full time", or it can remain "empty time" – just time!

Time could be an opportunity for Growth: a door that has been opened for the Grace of God to lead us toward Him… or just an opaque wall, not letting any light through, deceiving us with some false shiny lights.

Are we focused on Holiness? Are we focused on true time? On the true meaning of time? Do we find happiness in everyday life? Are we really growing? Are we using true tools of discernment in order to see through the opaque wall of life and time?

Can we Talk About Holiness?

Question: Yves Congar has the following quote from Fr. Emile Mersch in his book:

*"Wherever humans act as humans, in everything that Christians do – even the best, in all that ecclesiastical leaders do, even the most dignified, human weakness and human malice and the trace of human sins inevitably betrays itself – and does so often. The saints themselves do not totally escape from these bad moments **except at the moment of their full spiritual maturity** when they're dying. Grace, as we ought to believe, should preserve the pastors of the church and even more their most important actions, but it does not suppress their failures – that would be to suppress their humanity. There is then, even there, beyond authentic faults, the interference of selfish viewpoints and worldly calculation even in the perspective of the most apostolic persons; there are prejudices and unconscious ignorance, vanity that renders people inattentive, touchiness that nourishes unacknowledged grudges, prideful stubbornness which insists upon respect for the role they play, impotence to have and to keep a genuinely right intention in the spirit of true humble abnegation, etc"* ("True and False Reform in the Church" by Yves Congar, p. 84, 2011. The quote is taken from "La théologie du Corps mystique", vol. 1, p. 368.)

I know that in Proverbs (Pr. 24:16) it states that the just man sins seven times a day but I am trying to square all this with *Union with God*. I can understand the part of human weaknesses but when he states, "human malice and the trace of human sins inevitably betrays itself – and does so often" I am struggling. I would have thought **the purification would have taken care of this** for the Union with God to take place. When the saint dies, he/she dies of love so the moment of death can be seen as a moment of their full spiritual maturity but surely human malice and human sins don't feature often?

Answer: To a certain extent both of you are on the same wavelength. Fr. Mersch says: *"The saints themselves do not totally escape from these bad moments **except at the moment of their full spiritual maturity** when they're dying."*

69

The saints before they became saints are not saints yet. One needs to observe when and how the change occurs, especially as described by St. John of the Cross: going from the human mode to the divine mode, during the dark night of the spirit. Fr. Mersch says: "except at the moment of their full spiritual maturity…." The maturity is what you are alluding to: when purification is finished, and when they are transformed in God, united with Jesus and are moved by the Holy Spirit. In this sense you both are saying the same thing. Your slight disagreement is elsewhere. There are still two more points to underline:

1- Fr. Mersch adds immediately after "full spiritual maturity": "when they are dying". As you can see, "full spiritual maturity" for him is just before dying. He is writing in 1936. The knowledge we had at that time (and we still have the same knowledge today), about the part of the journey of spiritual life that follows union with God, covers a shorter "span of time" than that which Fr. Louis Guillet and I tend to find and explain. Fr. Marie Eugène would agree with Fr. Louis but he didn't have time to write the third volume of "I Want to See God" as he had wanted to do. It is important to acknowledge, therefore, that the majority of the Manuals of Spiritual Theology to date, state that *Union with God* is something almost rarely attainable and that if one attains it, he or she will live for only a brief time afterwards. Since Union is considered to be the maximum one can attain in this life on earth, it is thought that very soon after this one dies.

When, during the first lesson in Solid Foundations, i.e. "Goal and Stages of Spiritual Life", I threw out this question to the students: "Where would you place 'Union with God'?"… the answer to this question surprisingly was "in the middle" – so to speak – of the spiritual journey. By giving the above-mentioned answer, therefore, I am doing something totally new and extremely audacious. I, in fact, depart from all the manuals of Spiritual Theology except in the case of Fr. Louis Guillet OCD. In fact, nobody till now, except Fr. Louis (and the mind of Fr. Marie Eugene) has stated this! When I ask this question, I am upsetting the apple cart. It is simply revolutionary.

This is the reason for my having tried to demonstrate from the Gospels that we shouldn't place Union with God at the end of the life of the Apostles. We

70

should rather extend the time after Union with God to show how, in the life of the Apostles, "Union with God" occurred relatively earlier than what we can envisage. This seems to be unclear to theologians who have not said anything to this effect.

What I am proposing is that that more time passes after Union with Jesus, and this would certainly look far-fetched and extremely audacious to any person in the Church (Monks, Religious and Spiritual Masters, Spiritual Theologians)! Everybody accepts that we are called to holiness, but nobody imagines it is possible or can figure out what it really looks like and how we can reach it. Holiness remains very much a taboo subject. If one dares to tackle the subject by explaining or talking about it, he might be considered as unbalanced or lacking in humility.

Many saints had years and years of service after Union with God: take Mother Teresa of Calcutta, for example, who lived for 50 years after Union. Notwithstanding this, this type of analysis is extremely audacious in the eyes of the majority today. We still have many miles to go to accept viewing the journey this way. Maybe in 300 years it will be accepted!

Just think of it: many theologians, and amongst them the very famous, see that Thérèse, Mother Teresa, and many others, are still in the latter period of their spiritual life, in their purification time (Dark Night) when they die, while in fact they are enduring a different type of trial, i.e. participating in the Lord's Passion. If we follow the common opinion, i.e. that they are still being purified, it means that they would have died without even having finished their main purification! Shocking, no? We still have a way to go in order to really thoroughly understand the spiritual journey, and to do so in a practical way.

So, if many see these great saints as being in the *Dark Night* toward the end of their life, you can easily understand why Fr. Mersch considers that purification finishes (if it does) toward the end of the life of a human being. 2- Let us now see things from another perspective. Say for instance they have reached Union with God and still have plenty of time ahead to serve the Lord. Would they fall? Would they sin? Theoretically yes, of course they can. Being united doesn't remove freewill. Think of Adam: he was united to

71

God and still chose to sin. St. Teresa of Avila speaks about Solomon's sin toward the end of his life (marrying foreign women and worshiping their gods) in the Seventh Mansions. She talks about suffering, trials, wars, in the Seventh Mansions.

But of course, I would recommend the careful reading of St. John of the Cross and see his description of the transformation that occurs in the way the mind, memory and will start to operate, under the divine modality of action of the Holy Spirit. The only one who can save us from going astray in our interpretations is St. John of the Cross, and he needs to be read properly. The course "Reading and Studying St. John of the Cross" aims at that.

Similarly, St. Therese invents a new expression: faults (not sins) to describe what occurs to her (and this is after Union). She falls, out of weakness. But what needs to be "seen" is how one bounces back after falling. This point deserves careful study and analysis. The soul at this juncture has been greatly transformed so that the bouncing back is completely different.

In conclusion, I will return to and emphasise your observation on how the first lesson of the Solid Foundations Course, i.e. Goal and Stages of Spiritual Life, is a fundamental lesson that supports the entire structure of the Course and of any teaching in Spiritual Life or Spiritual Theology. Your observation is both accurate and noteworthy.

The more time passes, I find there is a greater necessity for the renewal of Theology to take place, in the direction of Spiritual Theology, if the notion of the Spiritual Journey is to be fully integrated into it. Therefore any topic addressed by Theology should be particularly considered in the light of the point reached by the human being on his or her spiritual journey. This is particularly so as each stage of growth will offer a different perspective, a new light and depth on any given subject.

The truth is that any discussion about the Spiritual Journey cannot be undertaken because most people fail to comprehend what it really entails, or what the stages of growth mean in practical terms, or more significantly they fail to see their impact on their lives as Christians. Thus, we admit in general terms that Jesus is the Way, but even this truth is understood in a lifeless way, namely, that He comes into our life, walks with us, consoles us, guides us, is our role model... and that is it. There is no journey of growth! Admittedly there is a journey, but it about journeying only, walking so to speak, but this has no effect on our spiritual growth and transformation. The result is that even the essential notion that Jesus is the Way to the Father, is understood in a very static way with no resultant growth. Therefore, when those who think in such a way are faced with the real notion of growth, transformation, and purification, they find it very difficult to absorb these. They most certainly try to understand, but the journey itself does not necessarily take root in their mind and spirit. Consequently, what is written in the old manuals of Spiritual Theology seems remote, including the very concept of 'holiness' itself! Sometimes it can even follow a pattern of behaviour, but will not necessarily be a transformative journey. The unfortunate outcome is that many find it acceptable to mix purification with union and then to return to purification... to add a little bit of this and a little bit of that! The message is clearly that the notions involved have not been properly understood. (See the Course: Reading and Studying St. John of the Cross)

The conclusion to this problem is, that there is a fundamental need to offer to the Adult Formation in the Parish, this notion of spiritual growth, with its goal and its stages. Even if at first one finds it all simply gibberish, at least the faith mind-set will have been shaped from the very beginning, to prepare the understanding for the deep changes that will come later, namely, when Jesus will enter in a definite way, a stronger and clearer way into their life.

The Journey of The Gift of Ourselves to God

Question: How can I completely give/surrender myself to Him; I insist on "completely", that is, to accept His will with pleasure & with a heart at peace?

Answer: Maybe you didn't expect how important this question is and how it needs a long explanation! It is the basic question for us Christians, and we need to understand clearly a very basic element of our life, which is at the heart of the Gospel. I have divided my explanation into 7 parts. They are all linked together, and they are all equal in their importance and need to be understood carefully, in order to see the whole picture!

1- Introduction

As a starting point I would like to recall the deep meaning of Marriage according to the western theological Tradition: "it is the mutual gift of a man and a woman!" He gives himself to her, and she gives herself to him. This is the very essence of marriage for the western Church! So, as you see, it is a mutual gift of themselves.

Let us now understand in a deep and truthful way what Jesus is for us! The Son of God, came from heaven, became a man, and gave himself to each of us on the Cross! He gave Himself totally on the Cross, to you, to me, to every human being! This is very important! This is why He is called the Groom, the Spouse! Because He gave everything to you! He would like you to be his Bride, so He invites you… He calls you, deep deep in your heart! So, your reply to Him, your response to His amazing Love, is to give yourself to Him, totally!

Do you understand the context of your question?! You are asking me to explain how you can answer fully to His Divine Love, in order to give yourself totally to Him! So the context is His Love to you, His call to you, deep in your heart! He is seducing you, He has lit a spark of his love in your heart! So your immediate reaction, once you became aware of His love and his call, is to reply to Him, to give Him the maximum: everything totally, in order to follow Him, to love Him, totally, and equally!

When you were young, your Godparents presented you in the Church to Jesus, and they immersed your being, totally, in Him. They did it for you, because they thought this is a good thing to give you: God himself. This very moment of Baptism, is in fact the Seed of the realisation of this Divine Marriage between you and Jesus! In fact, Baptism is an immersion in Jesus, in his Being. It is the gift of yourself to Him. So in fact your real Divine Marriage actually happened a few years ago!

But it is in a form of a Divine seed in you. The spark of this Seed has been revived in you recently, and in fact you want to realise this Seed in its fullness: you want to deepen what happened during your baptism: receiving Jesus fully, and giving yourself totally to Him! A Divine exchange!

2- Renewal of Baptism

Once we meet Jesus as adults, once we hear his call in our heart, once we understand that He wants us totally for himself, we feel the urge to give Him everything! We do not succeed in that immediately! We might start first to be "intellectually" convinced that this is the right thing to do, but we find that we are unable, by our will, to do it! The mind knows this is the right thing but the will is still too weak, the slave of many things, and dependant on them!

So, now, we begin more determinedly to keep contact with Jesus, by reading his words in the Gospel and putting them into practice! We feel then that our will is altogether strengthened and freed from the slavery of the world and of the flesh. Then after weeks/months we reach a point where we feel that we can freely leave everything and follow Him. This doesn't mean at all that we really have to leave physically our actual state to enter another state (become a nun or something like that) not at all! It is just through the will, that interiorly we feel freer to follow Jesus, to do what He wants from us! We can very well remain in the world, without changing a great deal in what we do, but, interiorly, we feel already different, and willing to follow Him. This step is very important in our life, and in way, it is the renewal of our Baptism, but as adults!

You can consider this step as a gift of yourself, and truly it is! But, it is just the beginning of a long journey that will lead us to much greater things: the mutual gift where all our being is transformed in Jesus! The spiritual marriage, or union with God, on earth! Ok?

3- To give yourself totally

In order to understand the dynamism of the gift of yourself to Him and its realisation I would like to use an image/symbol: the log and the fire! The log as you know is a piece of wood we put in the fireplace! We are the log and Jesus is the Fire! Ok?

a) To give myself

To give myself in fact is to put the log into contact with the Fire, to repeat this operation, and to try to remain in contact as long as possible with the Fire. So here, as you see, it is an act, and it depends on us. This will allow the Fire to burn the log more and more and transform it into fire! Ok?

b) To give myself totally

To give myself totally now means to reach the state or the step/stage where the log is totally transformed into the fire. So, as you see, this is the result of a). It is the result of the repeated (daily) gift of myself. It is the result of a repeated act (a). Ok? In a), everyday I give myself to God, I renew the gift of myself, using my freedom. This daily gift doesn't transform me immediately, but it helps me take one step! This step is important! You remember the ball of wool. If Jesus holds one end of the wool, He will pull all of it totally towards himself. I just need to put into His hands, daily, the end of the string! Renewing, everyday the gift of myself (an act I can perform) helps me to keep the log in contact with the Fire. So, one day, the whole log will be transformed into the Fire: the gift of myself will be total in this case!! Even if the daily gift of myself to Him is also total, "total" here is different from total there! What I can give today, is all myself, but what He can transform is a small part (one step). It is total on my part, but my growth is step by step!

So I don't have to be disappointed if I give today or one day, everything, but I don't find myself completely transformed! The new creature in me grows, day after day! Not in one shot!

As I also said, we need to remember that while climbing the Divine Mountain (Jesus) we don't have to be disappointed if we have to climb only one step each day ("being faithful to the little" as the Gospel says)! We need to remember that by giving ourselves totally today, we climb one step, but in a way, the whole mountain is contained in this small step! We never have to underestimate the total importance of today's step!

Keeping the contact between the Fire and the log, keeps the contact between Jesus and us, so He renews us, everyday, and transforms us into Him. Step by step.

4- How can we start this journey, how can we reach the goal: total gift of ourselves?

The main way to realise the daily gift of myself to Jesus (a gift that lets me grow and be transformed in Him) is to renew daily the desire to put Him in the first place. In fact I need to use my freedom every day in order to choose Him. Remember that all the Creation belongs to Him, heaven and earth, but only one thing doesn't belong to Him: your freedom of choice, your will, your desire! He will never step into them, they are yours! In fact nobody can touch them! You are the only owner of them, and God never touches them! But if you love Him, if you want to give yourself to Him, you need to use this treasure that belongs to you. He gave you the freedom, and will never take it back. This is your treasure, it is yours! You need to use it, and use it abundantly, in order to grow! But every time you use it, you still own it for the following time! So remember that everyday you are a free person in the eyes of God, and that in order to love Him really, you need to make use of this freedom. You are the paradise of God, as the Bride is the Paradise of the Divine Spouse! But in this Paradise, there is a tree God swore to himself not to touch: your freedom! So remember the power of seduction God put into you: the use of your freedom, to choose Him, to put Him in first place!

In order to put him in first place by an act (this is the good use of your freedom), you are invited to a) listen to Him, and to b) immerse yourself in Him, everyday! To listen is an act, and to immerse yourself in Him is also another type of act! They depend on you! God gives you always his grace in order to perform them!

a) To listen to Him is a act that I described when I explained the *Lectio Divina*. In fact in order to listen to Him one needs to offer all his being, and be ready to listen to whatever He wants to say. We need to put all our being under His light, so He can shed his light on a place in our soul that He wants to change! As you see, the Lectio Divina is the first and highest way to choose God, to give ourselves daily to Him! An efficient Lectio Divina is where his word received today, is put into practice with His grace today!

b) To immerse ourselves! This is the second highest act of gift of ourselves we can realise! In fact, as I taught you, in order to immerse ourselves in Jesus, our Divine Ocean of Love, the Divine Oven of Fire, we need to give ourselves to Mary, to put all of ourselves, all of our life into her hands, like a little child ("in order to enter the kingdom of God we need to become like children," if not, we can't enter! Mary is the mother of these children because She is the mother of each one of us, the mould of the Divine Jesus, and of our Divine new being!). Being immersed in God, helps our roots to be transformed into the Fire of God. Because the log I was speaking about earlier, is in fact a whole tree. The visible part of the tree is transformed by the Fire of the Word of God in Lectio Divina! While the deep roots of the tree (the heart) can only be transformed in God, by this type of prayer, where all our being is immersed in God (especially our roots).

In the Mass we have two types of "goods"/foods, and Lectio and the Prayer of the Heart are just an extension of these 2 types of food, so that we become transformed in God!

Remember that a) opens the gate to b).

Remember too the beautiful definition of love by Saint Thérèse of the Child Jesus: to love is to give everything [to God] and to give ourselves [to Him]. So if I say to God: I love you (First commandment: "you shall love God with all your heart, all your energy, all your intelligence…") this implies that I am invited to give flesh to this love, to realise it!

5- Difficulties

Of course, in this journey, we can feel the difficulty of repeating the gift of ourselves to God, we can find also that it is not easy to do listen to Jesus and do his will. Why? Because the old creature in us (the "old man") is still alive! The log is not yet totally transformed into the Fire! And the old creature in us doesn't like the Light of God! The "muscles" of our new being too are not well used to do the will of God, so we can feel that it seems difficult to walk with Jesus! In order to help this situation, it is important to remember that we don't have to look at the whole log, and despair! We need to concentrate only on the act to do today, and be very happy that we did it! This is the biggest grace God gives us every day! It is sometimes tiring to look at the top of the mountain, and see how far we might be! But this is not good! We need to concentrate on each step to do it correctly, and when we look to the mountain we need to feel the energy of God invading our being and encouraging us to continue to climb!

We need to remember always that it is a progressive journey and that God is very happy to see us do today's act! One act a day, makes Him happy (one new act each day, and we don't loose the other acts we have already done). We need to accept humbly not to arrive at the top of the mountain in one day. We need to accept humbly to bear this "burden". We need to bear the "old creature" in us. In fact they are both, the new and the old creature in us, like in a battle! We are like a pregnant woman with twins in her womb. We need to be patient and accept to grow step by step! Jesus said that our new being grows like a tree! And a tree needs weeks, months and years to grow properly, and to be deeply rooted! We need to remember that we please God immensely if we concentrate on today's step, by doing it!

The presence of the "old man" in us, still alive, his heaviness, his laziness, inconsistency don't have to push us into despair, but to patience! Our old heart is an old heavy stone, and God is removing it, slowly! Patience! Courage, perseverance!

We need to see that Jesus is growing in us!

We need to look at what we have achieved by his grace, and thank God for it.

We don't have to look back…

We don't have to look at the old man in us! He will die by himself! We don't have to bother to look at him of fight against him!

Humility: the Gospel reminds us that we need to come down (in fact "climbing" is in fact a "digging", a "coming down"), to make ourselves small, like a little child.

Mary, as I said, is the Mould of the new man in us. We need to give her every burden every worry, to put ourselves in her Arms. Even our desire to love Jesus, to give ourselves totally to Him, we need to put them into her hands, so She can keep our desire in a safe place, and help it grow and persevere! We can lose the graces we receive! Our heart leaks! But if we give Her everything, if we give Her our spiritual life, the graces we receive, She can keep them safe! Her Heart keeps everything, and never loses any grace received! She does that also for us! In fact we can become very easily the "owners" of our spiritual life, of our growth. So, it is good to remember real divine humility, and give everything to the real mother of the Humble, the Humble Mary! God looked to her humility, like a divine valley; She is able to keep all the water the grace in her Heart and let it fructify.

It is good to renew our purpose to give ourselves to Jesus in the hands of Mary. She keeps our promises safe! She immerses us in Him.

6- The stages of the realisation of the gift of ourselves

Before continuing on to the new step of the explanation I would like to remind you of the first point I mentioned! The framework of all that we are saying is that: the love of Jesus for you is total, unique, exclusive, jealous (divine jealousy). This is always the starting point! He is looking for you! He gave himself to you, totally, on the Cross! This is the essence of Baptism, the essence of our being as Christians! This is the deepest meaning of the Cross. The Cross is the place where the Divine Spouse gave himself totally to the Bride! So giving yourself to Him totally will be a spiritual marriage with Him – on earth!

Spiritual marriage is the realisation of the Divine Seed of the Baptism! The full mutual gift of you and Jesus!

Now, let us look at this new point: the stages of the gift of ourselves to Jesus! In fact, as I said, it is a journey. There are many steps that mark our growth in Jesus! The more the log is taken/transformed by the Fire, the more it goes through different stages/steps. We can mention 7 steps at least:
1- In the beginning we have a divine attraction to Jesus. We are seduced by him!

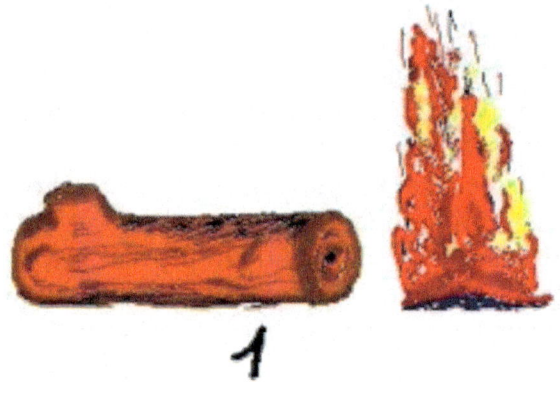

But we are very weak and not constant. We need to strengthen our inner being, our will in God, we need to be regular and to persevere. We choose Jesus every time, and put Him in the first place. It is like a battle/war… and persevering will give us a first Victory.

2- After having persevered in listening to God every day, and being constant, and practising this immersion in Jesus, we reach what we call the union of wills! Our will is united to the will of God (not all our being, but a central part of it). We take the first big step towards Peace! We experience it like a first big victory, like coming out of Egypt (the Exodus)! We are more attached to Jesus, in a stronger way, and our will is better rooted in Him.

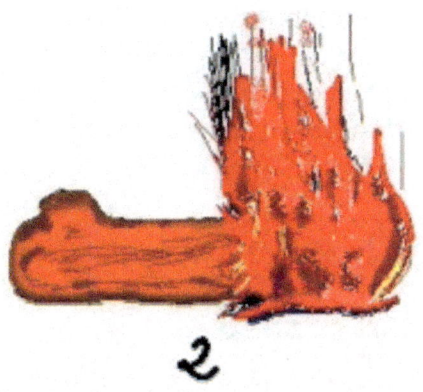

2

3- Then after this step we seem to make a new start, in order to reach a total purification of the soul (emotions, feelings etc..) and of the spirit (the ego). The Love of Jesus, takes now very seriously the gift of ourselves and performs a thorough purification /transformation of our being into His!

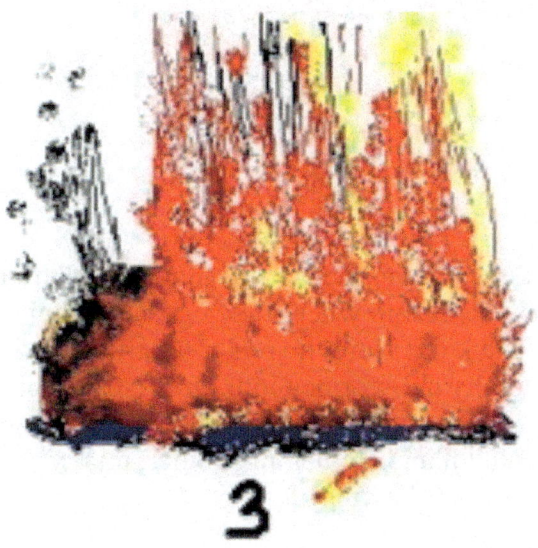

3

4- After this radical step, we reach finally a much greater peace, that reaches the bottom of our heart. From now starts what we call the spiritual "engagement" between Jesus and us! We have been able to say a first "yes" with all our being purified! It may seem strange to say that, because until we reach this step we have already given ourselves to Him hundreds of times and said "yes" to Him hundreds of times! But here, in fact it is different, the whole being, (including the roots) can say "yes", in a pure/total way! The Fiancée now is prepared by the Holy Spirit for the Marriage! Her dress (spiritual dress) is decorated/adorned by the Holy Spirit with many graces and precious stones, so to speak, so she can be ready for the wedding! It is a joyful preparation time.

5- Now comes the delicate, most beautiful moment where the Son of God receives His Bride in His Room where they exchange their "yes" with each other!!!!!! Secret of the king! Here the real total gift of herself is realised in fullness! The log is totally transformed into Fire, and participates fully in the operations of the Fire. She is his and He is hers! Full possession of each other! She belongs to Him and He belongs to her, totally and truly! She can give God to God! Secret of the king!

6- A new step starts where the Bride starts to bring children to the Divine Spouse! Because it is not enough to be united to Him, in one, she needs to have children! The log, totally on Fire, starts to Sparkle Divine sparkles, she starts to give God to many children!!! Another Secret of the king!! A long period of service starts and is full of gifts from her to Him!! In fact, each child is a gift from her (transformed into the Fire and moved by it) to HIM.

She gives Him supreme joy! This 6th step in fact can be divided into many different steps, but it is not our purpose today to discuss them!

7- The moment of Death, is in fact one more act of love from her, where the Holy Spirit pulls the Precious Stone of her soul and spirit and plunges her into the immense ocean of the Divinity. This is the Christian death: a full immersion in God, fuller even than that of the spiritual marriage, even if there are no, basically, other stages! This is a fuller possession of God.

You can very easily imagine a drawing where you have a log and a fire. You can easily imagine 5 steps at least of the evolution (growth) of the fire, transforming more and more the log into its very nature!

7- Conclusion

To conclude my answer we need to remember that the main way to give yourself to Jesus totally is to look to meeting Him everyday, to Listen to Him daily, and to be immersed in Him also everyday! This is the food that nourishes the growth of the gift!

Renewing daily the gift of ourselves, putting all our life in his hands, makes us take a step per day, and a greater part of our being is given to Him in fact (is transformed into Him).

May Our Lady keep your generosity in her safe hands and help you persevere everyday.

§§§

Question: *How can I know that God wants this priest to be my Spiritual Guide starting from now? Are there any signs He can give? If yes, like what?*

Answer: The real Spiritual guide and Father, and Spiritual Master, is the Holy Spirit. He speaks to you and want always to guide you and to speak to you. He likes to speak to you through human beings! I like to say always: God became flesh in order to talk to us through the flesh. Even if Jesus is on the right hand of the Father, He still likes to speak to us through the flesh!

His flesh is Nature, His flesh is the Bible, his flesh can be any human being! He guides you, in order for you to grow. Don't put yourself in the hands of a human being! Put yourself in the Hands of the Holy Spirit and He will guide you. When you listen to a man/woman don't listen to the human part of him/her, listen to God, to your real Master, and pray to Him!

We don't find the best Spiritual Director, but we find the right one for now! "For now" because we may need another priest after a while! Because very rarely can one priest lead you to achieve the whole journey! What I described above it not really known by the priests! They don't learn it (it is not their fault) when they do theology! So be careful into whose hands you put yourself, and you need to put the priest under trial! God warns us saying: that you will become the image of your Spiritual Father! Because you receive from his spirit! And God says, you can hardly find one in one thousand! It is the Bible that says this!

This is why it is a bit difficult to answer to you!

You need to distinguish between confession (the sacrament of the forgiveness) and spiritual direction! It is not the same thing at all! Any priest can confess you and give you the forgiveness of your sins, but not any priest or monk can lead you to Union with God!

Pray, pray and pray!! This is the only way, and be attached only to God, even if you seek confirmation "through the flesh" as I say! Both are necessary: being attached totally to God (not to the man), and seeking confirmation "through the flesh"! iI your intention is right, you will always find the right person, the right advice along your way! And pray a lot for the priests!

Questions on the Union With God

When should we start to pay attention to "bearing fruits"?

In order to address the above-mentioned, I will start by answering the questions that follow.

1- Question: *During <u>the first lesson of the First level Course</u>, you said that the fruits come after Union with Jesus. "Union with" Jesus can be compared to a tree that reaches maturity, after which the tree is supposed to start bearing fruits. Similarly, Union with Jesus is like marriage and after which one has children. My question is: while we are in the state of purification (in order to reach "Union with Jesus") could one start paying attention to "bearing fruits"? The fear is that the fruit will not be really fruit, because the self who is giving that fruit **is not pure** yet... Therefore, should we refrain from producing fruits, thinking that we are still in the purification phase?*

1- Answer: It depends on what you call "fruits". If you mean by "fruits" the time "after union, the union with Jesus" (Spiritual Marriage), then you are right: there is a difference between one act made after Union and all the acts made before. On this St. John of the Cross says: "an act of pure love [i.e. made after purification] is more precious in the eyes of God and the soul, and more profitable to the Church, than all other good works together [done before], though it may seem as if nothing were done" (*Spiritual Canticle* B,

Stanza 29, Introduction) because the act after union is "informed" (the form is given by) the Holy Spirit. Of course, St. John of the Cross' statement is quite strong, and it should encourage us to do all what we can in order to grow. This is exactly what St. Thérèse of the Child Jesus did when she read that passage.

But, from another angle, "purification" is a sacred work and should be considered as a goal in itself, for through it, we reach union; it is of course an *intermediate* goal. The phase of purification can thus be perfectly considered as a "fruit". Indeed, each step in the phase of purification is a "fruit".

From the start, when we add to this Listening to the Daily Word of God, we are *de facto* listening and putting into practice the Daily Word received. In turn the real fact of putting into practice this Word is in itself a Fruit, **a fundamental fruit**, a real change, a real step ahead, and this happens **right from day one**. But if we do not do it, dreaming of a spiritual future is pointless. This is the condition *sine quae non* in order to reach the different phases of purification that follow as well as the later steps.

So maybe, it would be better to give an additional understanding of the concept of "fruit". "Loving our neighbour" for instance doesn't wait until we reach Union with Jesus – definitely not! But, certainly, the quality of our love after union is enormously different and exceedingly better. But is important to bear in mind that if we don't start from day one to love our neighbour, we will never reach union. Hence, two undertakings must be underlined: first, the effort made in order to grow (the ascending curve) and then the more direct effort made in order to bear direct fruits. Each, in its own timing is vital, essential and non-negotiable.

What about sins and weaknesses?

2- Question: *Even after Salvation achieved by the work of Jesus on the Cross, what about the sins and weaknesses that stand in the way of our becoming a real human being, namely, returning to the original likeness of God in which we were created? In other words, how can we understand the relationship between Salvation and actual sins?*

2- Answer: The deep analysis of the spiritual journey shows us that there are real changes in the human being. Bad habits come to an end, sins stop… I mean serious sins. When the Power of the Resurrection of Jesus enters us, real change commences, otherwise, there would be no growth, no transformation and no purification. The very definition itself of the word "purification" highlights the process of creating a real change: here we see an old "form" in us is taken away by the Holy Spirit and is replaced by a holier "form" instead. A real change happens, therefore sins and weaknesses (that are in fact sins) do tend to disappear, starting from the lower and more materialistic ones.

Having said that, many Christians don't believe in real change, they don't believe that a real change can occur in them. Admittedly, we don't change our nature, or our character and temperament, but sins do disappear. Furthermore, if the human being on earth doesn't change, this wouldn't be real Christianity; this wouldn't convey the message of the Gospel. Some Christians do believe that once Jesus covers us with His Blood that's enough and this compensates for anything we do later; in other words, we remain roughly as we were. This is a wrong understanding of the application of Salvation to us. All the Christian Masters of Spiritual Life do state clearly that the human being changes, and they do go on to describe the steps of this deep inner (and external) change.

Let us also be mindful of the difference between the *inclination/tendency to sin* and to sin itself. Let me explain: if I see a lovely chocolate pudding, yummy, I'll feel a certain natural inclination/attraction toward it. This is not a sin! Baptism doesn't remove the inclination to sin, rather it is left in us for the ensuing *spiritual warfare* that will generate real growth and change.

The same is true of the case of **weaknesses that are not sins**, but are rather based on character or temperament. One must read the great St. Thérèse of the Child Jesus who revolutionised *Spiritual Life* and *Spiritual Theology*. Similarly, if we correctly read St. John of the Cross, we will find the same teaching. She introduced the possibility of having errors, faults (fautes) that are not sin, and that don't sadden God. Making this difference is subtle but important.

More than this is the fact that spiritual growth (purification) doesn't generate in us greater strength, but by contrast greater weakness. Jesus says in the Gospel: "blessed the poor in spirit" and to St. Paul who was asking him to remove a "thorn" from his flesh, thinking that that would be "perfection" Jesus likewise says: I rejoice and work in your weakness – this means: you'll remain weak, and therefore my Grace will work better in you, so you will not lean on your new strength but on my Grace. This is a different understanding of Perfection. We should renew our understanding of "perfection", of "holiness" – the real goal we are seeking. We are heading toward spiritual growth in the discovery of our weakness, and a growing spiritual experience of the Mercy of God. As can be seen, then, many of our ways of understanding, many elements of spiritual life, will be turned **upside-down**, during our spiritual growth.

Are there sins after Union?

3- Question: *After the Union with Jesus, does sin still exist in the succeeding phases?*

3- Answer: God is Freedom. Jesus is God. When a person reaches Union with Jesus, one doesn't have less freedom, but more freedom. Certainly, the person is transformed in God, in Jesus, but this doesn't deprive the person of his/her freedom. Remember Adam: he was close to God, in the beginning, and he still sinned.

When St. Theresa of Avila speaks about union with Jesus, she mentions the example of Salomon. He started his spiritual life well but ended very badly worshiping the gods of his foreign wives, just demonstrating very clearly that nobody is exempt from the possibility of sinning – God forbid of course. During this lifetime we have a body, we have freedom, we can perform acts: therefore, we can sin. This is why Jesus said that we need to persevere "till the end", and that nothing is guaranteed. Of course, nobody wants to sin, neither Jesus nor we desire this. This is also why we need the *final perseverance,* and we need to remain in the Grace of God till our final hour as is so significantly petitioned at the end of the Hail Mary: "pray for us, …, at the hour of our death. Amen"

What is perfection?

4- Question: *Can we picture Union with God?*

4- Answer: Jesus explains to us some aspects of the Union with God when He says: *"""You have heard that it was said, 'You shall love your neighbour and hate your enemy.' **44** But I say to you, love your enemies, bless those who curse you, do good to those who hate you, and pray for those who spitefully use you and persecute you, **45** that you may be sons of your Father in heaven; for He makes His sun rise on the evil and on the good, and sends* *rain on the just and on the unjust. 46 For if you love those who love you, what reward have you? Do not even the tax collectors do the same? 47 And if you greet your brethren only, what do you do more than others? Do not even the tax collectors do so? 48 Therefore you shall be perfect, just as your Father in heaven is perfect."* (Mt. 5:48)

However, what is perfection? According to Jesus' words, then, perfection is to love both your friends and your enemies. Love must flow from an inner abundance, springing from our hearts. The one who believes in Jesus opens himself to the Abundance of Spirit flowing out of God. Accepting Jesus' Gift (the Holy Spirit) transforms our heart. The Holy Spirit puts Jesus at the centre of our heart, so that we can say: "it's not I who live, but Jesus lives in me" (St. Paul) as well as acts through me and with me.

Jesus' pierced heart is open all the time, from which springs forth the Holy Spirit, unconditionally, to everybody. For this reason, one of the most common images used to translate this openness, this unconditional abundance is the Sun. Jesus is our real Sun, radiating continuously upon us. The perfection of God is a perfection of Love, "Love is to give oneself" for, by its very nature Love gives of itself. This Perfection of God's nature bears within it "abundance" and "unconditional" love. The very nature of God is to give, unconditionally. God loves because He is Love. He finds the reason to love in Himself (not in us). The power of love, this capacity to love, this ever-flowing unconditional abundance is what characterises the very nature of God, his holiness and his perfection.

We often tend to imagine perfection in an aesthetical way, like a Greek statue, with no errors in its forms, proportions, beauty, expression, and numbers. By contrast, however, we are called to change our vision of God's perfection and holiness. Our initial idea of perfection is rather a projection, an artificial form of how we imagine it – I call it: perfection as expressed in a Greek statue. But is this how God understands perfection? We need to allow God to show us His true nature, his love and mercy and where perfection lies. St. Paul is a very good example here (see 2 Cor 12:1-10): he wanted hi source of struggle to be removed (the images he uses is: to remove a thorn from his side), but God said to him that His grace works better in Paul's weakness! Here is the paradox, perfection seen by St. Paul is to have everything in him perfect, while perfection in the eyes of God is an increasing experience of our weakness supported by His utter Mercy. The difference between these two understandings is considerable.

This is essential, in order to be able to "imagine" or "picture" the perfection and holiness we are called to reach. "Union with God" is union with the One who is abundant, who loves unconditionally, and who finds in Himself an endless source of Love. He is the one who encompasses every being in the bosom of his Mercy. He is the "most low" (and not the "most high"), since His Being (Love), has brought Him to the lowest parts of humanity, to our darkness, just like rainwater that trickles down from a high mountain.

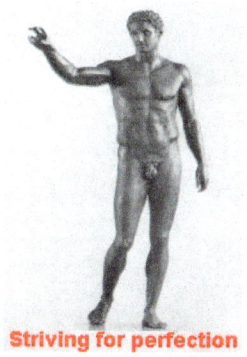

Striving for perfection

Perfection won't then be striving toward the strongest, the most powerful, the highest etc. that life has to offer, for perfection according to the true God is a downward process bearing the marks of Humility, Love, Compassion, Mercy that lead to eternal life.

It follows then that the greater in Mercy, is the one who is more united to God. The greater in patience, is the one more united to God.

The greater in humility and understanding, and excusing his brothers and sisters is closer to God.

The one who receives in his heart everybody, unconditionally, is the one who has been transformed into God.

93

Finally, taken as a whole, it can be seen that perfection is not a competition to reach the top of the highest mountain first. Neither is it the most aesthetic movement in our acts – as St. Paul wanted (see above). It is to have our heart replete with the Love of God and to love not with our own strength, but with God's.

Perfection is letting God transform our heart into His Heart, so we can be and act like Him. To paraphrase St. John who says it so eloquently: The one who believes will have streams of Living Water (the Holy Spirit) coming out of his bosom…. Streams of Mercy, of Love, of Compassion for his brothers and sisters.

The Meaning of Our Life: Bearing Children for Jesus

Summary: *The following article addresses a very common question: why doesn't God always convert the closest and dearest person to us? Six truths, six steps, are explored – often with quotes from the Scriptures and the Doctors of the Church – leading us to a deeper and wider understanding of such apparent silence from God. The latter steps introduce us into a new spiritual dimension where each step deserves to be meditated and gazed upon. It all leads to the discovery of a hidden dimension in our actual reality, in our daily life where each small act can now be transfigured into a new realm.*

Dear Jean,

*I am emailing you as it is easier, I think, to voice what I want to say this way, and I do need your help over a line I read in the gospel of St. John a day or two ago: "Yet there are some of you who do not believe. For Jesus had known from the beginning which of them did not believe and who would betray him." He went on to say, "This is why I told you that **no one can come to me unless the Father has enabled them**." (John 6:64-65)*

My understanding has been that God honours our free will and will not force Himself on us, so if we do not believe He accepts that. But the next verse is causing me the problem, namely: "no one can come to me unless it is granted him by my Father".

*I have understood this to mean that God chooses those to whom He wishes to give the faith, i.e., **He** calls us... **He** is the one who initiates always. But it has suddenly dawned on me that there are those whom God does not call. Like my poor husband. Why? I looked back at the gospels and I saw that Jesus did not perform miracles for everyone, and understood that as a human being He could only do a certain amount because of his human resources.*

How then does the Father, who is divine, choose not to give the faith to everyone?

I have accepted the Lord's will on this all my life without questioning it, and I still accept it, but I can't help wondering why. I know that following one's conscience, no matter what path you take (Buddhist etc) will ensure you will be acceptable in God's eyes…. But why does the Lord pick and choose those to whom He will reveal Himself when He wants all of us to be with Him in Paradise?

[…]

In Mary in this glorious Month of May,

N.

Thank you, N., for your email. Here is what I can say and I hope it can help you live your daily life better and obtain a better understanding as to why things are as they are.

1- God's Freedom and Mysterious Design

The main text that comes to your mind and to mine is St. Paul's one, underlining God's total and utter Freedom and Wisdom in choosing whoever He wants, when He wants. Choosing the persons, but also choosing the timing. St. Paul in fact suffered a lot to see his fellow Jewish people who didn't believe in Jesus. He even wished to be anathema (like going to Hell (Rm 9:3)) in order to have them discover Jesus. It is never easy to accept such a thing.

Here is the famous text:

"And it is not as that the word of God has failed. For not all who are of Israel, are these Israel. 7 Nor because they are seed of Abraham are all children. Rather, "In Isaac your offspring will be named." 8 That is, the children of the flesh, these are not children of God; but the children of the promise are regarded as offspring. 9 For this is the word of the promise: "At this time I will come, and to Sarah there will be a son."

*10 And not only so, but also Rebecca, having conception by one, Isaac our father, 11 for they not yet having been born nor having done anything good or evil, so that the purpose of God according to election might stand, 12 **not***

96

of works, but of the One calling, *it was said to her, "The older will serve the younger." 13 As it has been written: "Jacob I loved, but Esau I hated." 14 What then shall we say? Is there injustice with God? Never may it be! 15 For He says to Moses:*

"I will show mercy to whom I may show mercy,
and I will have compassion on whom I may have compassion."
16 So then, it is not of the willing, nor of the running, but of God showing mercy. 17 For the Scripture says to Pharaoh: "For this very purpose I have raised you up, so that I might show My power in you, and that My name should be declared in all the earth." 18 So then, He shows mercy to whom He wants, and He hardens whom He wants." (Rom 9:6-18)

For the majority God seems to wait, to delay. Hence the incomprehensible situation of bad people saying the Psalms yet also seeming to have a good life … oblivious of God. This is not the case of your husband of course.

In light of this underlining God's mysterious design and wisdom is fundamental. He has the initiative! No doubt about this! However, does this leave things totally in His Hands with us being totally passive?

2- God is Pleased

Thérèse, Manuscript A:

*"I wondered for a long time why God has preferences, why all souls don't receive an equal amount of graces. I was surprised when I saw Him shower His extraordinary favours on saints who had [2v°] offended Him, for instance, St. Paul and St. Augustine, and whom He forced, so to speak, to accept His graces. When reading the lives of the saints, I was puzzled at seeing how Our Lord **was pleased** to caress certain ones from the cradle to the grave, allowing no obstacle in their way when coming to Him, helping them with such favours that they were unable to soil the immaculate beauty of their baptismal robe. I wondered why poor savages died in great numbers without even having heard the name of God pronounced.*

*Jesus deigned to **teach me this mystery**. He set before me the book of nature; I understood how all the flowers He has created are beautiful, how the splendour of the rose and the whiteness of the Lily do not take away the perfume of the little violet or the delightful simplicity of the daisy. I understood that if all flowers wanted to be roses, nature would lose her*

*springtime beauty, and the fields would no longer be decked out with little
wild flowers.*

*And so it is in the world of souls, Jesus' garden. He willed to create great
souls comparable to Lilies and roses, but He has created smaller ones and
these must be content to be daisies or violets destined* **to give joy to God's
glances** *when He looks down at his feet.* **Perfection consists in doing His
will, in being what He wills us to be**.

I understood, too, that **Our Lord's love is revealed as perfectly** *in the most
simple soul who resists His grace in nothing as in the most excellent soul; in
fact, since* **the nature of love is to humble oneself**, *if all souls resembled
those of the holy Doctors who illumined the Church [3r°] with the clarity of
their teachings, it seems God would not descend so low when coming to their
heart. But He created the child who knows only how to make his feeble cries
heard; He has created the poor savage who has nothing but the natural law
to guide him. It is to their hearts that God deigns to lower Himself. These
are the wild flowers* **whose simplicity attracts Him**. *When coming down in
this way,* **God manifests His infinite grandeur**. *Just as the sun shines
simultaneously on the tall cedars and on each little flower as though it were
alone on the earth, so* **Our Lord is occupied particularly with each soul as
though there were no others like it**. *And just as in nature all the seasons are
arranged in such a way as to make the humblest daisy bloom on a set day,
in the same way,* **everything works out for the good of each soul**.*"*

3- We Need to Pray and Act for Conversion

If one only reads the text above one might think: ok, things are as they are,
we should leave them as they are. No! Jesus commanded us to spread the
Good News! Jesus invited us to pray to the Master of the harvest to call more
people to the harvest. We can't just stay passive, even if we have understood
something of God's wisdom above. He wants us to be part of His Plan, to
ask Him himself. He wants us to be his friends not his slaves! It is his friend
who knows His Heart, understands his heart and does his best to collaborate
with Him! It is we who must offer our sufferings for the conversion of others.

Dear Céline,

I cannot allow the letter to leave without joining a note to it. For this, I must steal a few moments from Jesus, but He does not hold it against me, for it is about Him that we speak together, without Him no discourse has any charms for our hearts... Céline, the vast solitudes, the enchanting horizons opening up before you must be speaking volumes to your soul? I myself see nothing of all that, but I say with Saint John of the Cross: "My Beloved is the mountains, and lonely, wooded valleys, etc." *And this Beloved instructs my soul, He speaks to it in silence, in darkness.... Recently, there came a thought to me which I have to tell my Céline. It was one day when I was thinking of what I could do to save souls, a word of the gospel gave me a real light. In days gone by, Jesus said to His disciples when showing them the fields of ripe corn: "Lift up your eyes and see how the fields are already white enough to be harvested," and a little later: "In truth, the harvest is abundant but the number of laborers is small, ask then the master of the harvest to send laborers." What a mystery!...* **Is not Jesus all-powerful?** *Are not creatures His who made them?* **Why, then, does Jesus say: "Ask the Lord of the harvest that he send some workers"? Why?...** *Ah! it is because Jesus has so incomprehensible a* **love for us** *that He wills that we* **have a share with Him in the salvation of souls. He wills to do nothing without us. The Creator of the universe awaits the prayer of a poor little soul to save other souls redeemed like it at the price of all His Blood.**

Our own vocation is not to go out to harvest the fields of ripe corn. Jesus does not say to us: "Lower your eyes, look at the fields and go harvest them." Our mission is still more sublime. These are the words of our Jesus: "Lift your eyes and see." See how in my heaven there are empty places; it is up to you to fill them, you are my Moses praying on the mountain, ask me for workers and I shall send them, I await only a prayer, a sigh from your heart!...

Is not the **apostolate of prayer**, *so to speak, more elevated than that of the word? Our mission as Carmelites is to* **form evangelical workers** *who will save thousands of souls whose mothers we shall be.... Céline, if these were*

*not the very words of our Jesus, who would dare to believe in them?... I find that **our share is really beautiful**, what have we to envy in priests?... How I would like to be able to tell you all I am thinking, but time is lacking, understand all I could write you!... [...]*
Your little Thérèse of the Child Jesus rel. carm. ind.

Here we see that we can't remain passive! Prayer and sacrifices offered out of love are, as they unfold, a powerful weapon of salvation, of spreading the Good News, of converting more people. We discover that not only has God the initiative to call people but that we have a part in this Sacred, Divine Work of Salvation. God depends on us, God needs us.

So, why is He not answering our prayers? Because He needs us to continue to pray till the end!

In this sense your husband "represents" mystically all the people Jesus is expecting you, as a true bride and mother, to bear for Him!! What a new dimension and depth of love this becomes.

4- We are Missionaries by Baptism

Because of our Baptism, we become "Priests in Christ" the High Priest. This means that we are called to pray, act and intercede for our brothers and sisters. Since we are baptised, we are called to be missionaries. "All the Laity Are Missionaries by baptism" says John Paull II (see *Redemptoris Missio* 71-72). Jesus' order to spread the Good News is not optional, it is a mandate. We are all called to take our share in it.

Mission – a requirement of the Church's catholicity

*849 **The missionary mandate**. "Having been divinely sent to the nations that she might be 'the universal sacrament of salvation,' the Church, in obedience to the command of her founder and because it is demanded by her own essential universality, strives to preach the Gospel to all men": "Go therefore and make disciples of all nations, baptizing them in the name of the Father and of the Son and of the Holy Spirit, teaching them to observe* *all that I have commanded you; and Lo, I am with you always, until the close of the age."*

850 **The origin and purpose of mission**. *The Lord's missionary mandate is ultimately grounded in the eternal love of the Most Holy Trinity: "The Church on earth is by her nature missionary since, according to the plan of the Father, she has as her origin the mission of the Son and the Holy Spirit." The ultimate purpose of mission is none other than to make men share in the communion between the Father and the Son in their Spirit of love.*

851 **Missionary motivation**. *It is from God's love for all men that the Church in every age receives both the obligation and the vigour of her missionary dynamism, "for the love of Christ urges us on." Indeed, God "desires all men to be saved and to come to the knowledge of the truth"; that is, God wills the salvation of everyone through the knowledge of the truth. Salvation is found in the truth. Those who obey the prompting of the Spirit of truth are already on the way of salvation. But the Church, to whom this truth has been entrusted, must go out to meet their desire, so as to bring them the truth. Because she believes in God's universal plan of salvation, the Church must be missionary.*

852 **Missionary paths.** *The Holy Spirit is the protagonist, "the principal agent of the whole of the Church's mission." It is he who leads the Church on her missionary paths. "This mission continues and, in the course of history, unfolds the mission of Christ, who was sent to evangelize the poor; so the Church, urged on by the Spirit of Christ, must walk the road Christ himself walked, a way of poverty and obedience, of service and self-sacrifice even to death, a death from which he emerged victorious by his resurrection." So it is that "the blood of martyrs is the seed of Christians."*

5- The Mystical Dimension of our Mission

God's Providence puts us in a certain place in life, with certain individuals. All this has a meaning. Let us try to see the relationship between our situation and our "mission" in life, or part of our mission.

Therefore, going even deeper in the same direction, I would say the following. We ourselves have an important and fundamental mystical dimension to discover, explore, deepen and live: the *Communion of Saints*. We are linked to our brothers and sisters: the ones who are already Christians and the ones who are not. We all have a portion of God's children entrusted to us, for whom He invites our help in applying His salvation. He wants us to be his true Bride. The bride becomes thereby a real mother for his children.

When we unite with Jesus, when we have a closer relationship with Him, we discover that Charity grows in us exponentially. God's love starts to push us out of our egoistical comfort zone, asking us to pray and care for a person – and not the person of our choice. Then He enlarges the action of His Charity in us and offers us more people. Then categories of people follow; then He reaches out to people who are really far from our perspectives: bad people, people who are bad in our eyes! He teaches us from within to love them, with His Love; He changes our mind and pushes us to cross many limits and boundaries in our understanding. It becomes a serious true love. The more charity grows in us the more we in charity reach out to more people and people far from Him. This is fundamental. We can't claim to know Jesus if His Charity and care for others, charity poured into us, doesn't reach more people and people who are distant from Him.

It is Charity which connects and unites us with these people! It ensures this invisible but true connection with our spiritual children. Through Charity we enter ever deeper into the Mystery of his Body and into the mysterious communication between us.

Plus, it is important to notice that our acts have implications for others. What we do, others benefit from! What a mystery. It is part of the "communion of saints"! This is fundamental, not optional. Entering into this mystery is vital. Now, you will notice that in order to teach us a very deep truth, the Lord, through certain prophets of the Old Testament (Ez 24:15 onward; Hosea 3), showed us how the wife of the Prophet had a mystical meaning also in that she represented God's people. When St. Paul says that Marriage relates to something much deeper than just husband and wife, that it incarnated essentially the relationship between Jesus and the Church, he is not saying anything different to what God had said through some of His prophets.

Therefore, what the Prophet will go through is in fact reflecting what is happening deeply between God and His People.

This is why each act between a Christian wife and a Christian husband, has a deep influence on the Church and the entire world.

When St. Paul says: *"So also husbands ought to love their wives as their own bodies. The one loving his wife loves himself. For no one at any time hated his flesh. But he nourishes and cherishes it [...]."* (Eph 5:28-29), he means that the wife is truly the husband's body and not an extension of it (and vice-versa), in the sense that there is a mystical dimension to the word "body" here!

St. Paul continues: *"Because of this, a man will leave his father and mother and be joined to his wife, and the two will be into one flesh." 32This mystery is great; but I speak as to Christ and as to the church."* (Eph 5:31-32)

It shows us here how in Christian marriage, that is, in the Sacrament, a mystical dimension has been introduced. The husband is much more than the husband and the wife becomes much more than the wife. They are carrying the mystery of salvation between the two of them, the mystery of salvation in which Christ saves the Church. It is a mystery of Salvation. This is why I tried to show that in the person of your husband there are thousands of people waiting their own salvation from you, of if you prefer, your taking your share of responsibility in the Salvation of your "mystical body". Accordingly, your husband becomes much more than your husband – he embodies the mystery of the people you are called to save.

We see, then, that the prophets Ezekiel and Hosea represented God, and their wives represented the people of God, the people He loves and wants to save. It is very deep. It is as if Marriage has introduced us into the depths of God's love for his people!

In this light we should consider each one of us as having a "mystical body", i.e. a number of children Jesus wants us to bear for Him! In this sense the deep communion one has with one's husband (they become "one" says the Bible when they marry) is a true mystery of salvation. This means that the husband or the wife (even if she is still 'rather far' from Jesus) represents a mystical dimension, a deep mystery, that represents not only the individually but also all the people we should work to bring to Jesus who are in the same state!

In this sense, the Growth of Charity introduces us into a very deep dimension where we communicate mysteriously but truly with others; where Jesus gives the bride the capacity to become a mother (this is one of the qualities of Divine Charity), where she finds that she has a "mystical body" to save, that the "Communion of Saints" is something more real than the visible life we lead.

Remember what Therese used to say when walking in huge pain during her last illness: "I walk for a Missionary". She saw and lived this responsibility, this invisible strong link, as a true Bride of Jesus. She knew that each of her acts had direct implications for others! That deep inside, like from another end, the house of her being had an inner open garden where she was able to communicate with thousands of people. She was led to discover that Union with Jesus was also a Union with a portion of His Mystical Body. She could not remain inactive or passive... she knew that each act of pure love, in Mary, had a mysterious power to bear children for God.

If, then, God allows your husband not to discover Jesus, maybe it is to keep you immensely motivated, and to have clear before your eyes that you have much to do still. Till the end.

Remember that because of the Communion of Saints, because of Charity, because of the Sacrament of Marriage, anything you do, is communicated to your husband and vice versa.

Let us draw closer to the one who had mastered this science in its fullness: Mary. Let us be carried by Her, by the infinite power of her Fiery Pray, to continue to elevate (unite) to God all his children scattered around the World.

6- The Power of the Fiery Prayer

I hope these explanations and horizons help you "see" better the meaning of the mystery in which you live, and the work Jesus is begging from you. But

104

please remember that the Fire of Love that comes from God is the only power that can lift, or bear children. This Fire of the Holy Spirit is fully acting in Mary. Let us just invoke her Fiery prayer, at the heart of the rosary, saying: "Pray for us" O "holy Mother of God" … The Rosary is to have recourse to Mary's Prayer, not to ours! She lifts the world. But just let us say: "Pray for us O Holy Mother of God" (the Hail Mary):

"All the saints have understood this, and more especially those who filled the world with the light of the Gospel teachings. Was it not in prayer that St. Paul, St. Augustine, St. John of the Cross, St. Thomas Aquinas, St. Francis, St. Dominic, and so many other famous Friends of God have drawn out this divine science which delights the greatest geniuses? A scholar has said: "Give me a lever and a fulcrum and I will lift the world." What Archimedes was not able to obtain, for his request was not directed by God and was only made from a material viewpoint, the saints have obtained [36v°] in all its fullness. The Almighty has given them as fulcrum: HIMSELF ALONE; as lever: PRAYER which burns with a fire of love. And it is in this way that they have lifted the world; it is in this way that the saints still militant lift it, and that, until the end of time, the saints to come will lift it." (Manuscript C, end)

7- You Will Save Your Husband

During apostolic times, when a married woman became Christian and her husband remained pagan, and wondered what to do, leave him or stay with him, St. Paul gave this advice:

*"If any brother has an unbelieving wife and she consents to dwell with him, let him not divorce her. 13 And if any woman has an unbelieving husband, and he consents to dwell with her, let her not divorce the husband. 14 For the unbelieving husband **is sanctified** in the wife, and the unbelieving wife **is sanctified** in the husband. Otherwise, your children are unclean; but now they are holy. 15 But if the unbeliever separates himself, let him separate himself. The brother or the sister is not under bondage in such cases. But God has called you into Peace. 16 For how do you know, wife, if **you will save** the husband? Or how do you know, husband, if **you will save** the wife?"* (1Co 7:12-16)

The individual is free, but he or she might as well stay with their husband or wife for you never know what can happen; maybe through the influence of the believer, and his prayers, he might win him over and he or she might be won over and convert. Of course, this is not your case at all. It is not also the case of many of you who might read this article. But what catches our attention here is something that goes deeper: St. Paul knows that a good influence, i.e. prayer, suffering (not abuse) and sacrifice can eventually be instrumental in the conversion, the salvation.

St. Monica prayed for years for her son. And in the end, God granted her the conversion of her son and he became one of the greatest saints and a doctor of the Church. Souls have a price. They have been redeemed by the Blood of God... is it not our privilege to give him some help?

In the final analysis do we ourselves want to be the only ones who are saved? Each act of love has two components: one that draws us toward God and one that through us draws our brothers to God. Both happen at the same time! This happens for any of the faithful, all the more reason does it happen for married people. Here is the explanation offered by St. Thérèse:

*"Mother, I think it is necessary to give a few more explanations on the passage in the Canticle of Canticles: "Draw me, we shall run," for what I wanted to say appears to me little understood. "No man can come after me, unless the FATHER who sent me draw him," Jesus has said. Again, through beautiful parables, and often even without using this means so well known to the people, He teaches us that it is enough to knock and it will be opened, to seek in order to find, and to hold out one's hand humbly to receive what is asked for. He also says that **everything we ask the Father in His name, He will grant it**. No doubt, it is because of this teaching that the Holy Spirit, before Jesus' birth, dictated this prophetic prayer: "Draw me, we shall run." What is it then to ask to be "Drawn" if not to be united in an intimate way to the object which captivates our heart? If fire and iron had the use of reason, and if the latter said to the other: "Draw me," would it not prove that it desires to be identified with the fire in such a way that the fire penetrate [36r°] and drink it up with its burning substance and seem to become one with it?*

Dear Mother, this is my prayer. **I ask Jesus to draw me into the flames of His love, to unite me so closely to Him that He live and act in me. I feel that the more the fire of love burns within my heart, the more I shall say: "Draw me,"** *the more also the souls who will approach me (poor little piece of iron, useless if I withdraw from the divine furnace),* **the more these souls will run swiftly in the odour of the ointments of their Beloved,** *for a soul that is burning with love cannot remain inactive."* (Manuscript C, end)

We can transform this important passage in this way: the more the Fire of love burns within my heart, the more I shall say "draw me", the more the soul of my husband who is attached to me, forming one mystical flesh – and the souls he mystically represents to me – will run swiftly in the odour of the ointments of their Beloved.

Yes. Amen.

You will save your husband. He is already saved. True, he doesn't experience what you yourself mystically experience, but he experiences it through you because you are one. When you lift him and with him lift all the persons he represents, you lift up all those whom Jesus wants to save. He/they will be saved by the help you offer to Jesus your Groom.

Looked at in the round you can see that Jesus blesses many people around you because of your love for Him, because you spread His Mercy. This is so even for people from other religions, because we are all in one community, receive blessings, as if we were in the wider circle of a communion of saints: they are potentially saved by Jesus on the Cross, waiting and begging you to help them, manifest in the new way you make your acts (i.e. with Mary's lifting Power). Each moment you try to live in Mary, immersed in Jesus, this benefits them. No doubt about it. We are all one Body – Jesus wants the salvation of All.

How to Emerge from a Lukewarm Spiritual Life

Recently I gave a talk on this subject, daring to address it for the first time from a completely different perspective to the surprise of many as a result. To cut to the chase I said: if you want to end your lukewarm Spiritual Life, devote more attention to the way you deal and manage your work life. Of course, this applies to everybody – to those who don't work, who can't work – with everyone being invited to make themselves busy, because "idleness is the mother of all vices". It is important not to create empty moments in your day, because the Devil takes advantage of them, finds space in you and starts to tempt you: thoughts start to go around in circles in your mind – and this tends to be dangerous and unhealthy.

Now, to return to the point: to pay greater attention to the way you commit to work and the quality of the way you deal with your work in a committed way, with attention to detail, accuracy, and quality.

First of all work takes up a large proportion of our day – one third! We can't neglect or discard a third of our existence.

Then too, we can't create a dichotomy between on the one hand "Work" and on the other hand our "Spiritual Life". Work is not essentially a burden imposed on us so that we can earn our living or a duty we can't escape from. As John Paul II used to say: *work makes us realise ourselves in life.* Therefore, we can't just live with the mental attitude: "I am waiting until I finish work in order to breath and do what I would like to do" be it hobbies, other business, rest, prayer. This would resemble a schizophrenic way of dealing with work and life. On the contrary there is a deep unity in our day and in our business-life. We can't exclude work from the values of our day, and even worse, we can't split our spiritual life into two parts: "alien pagan business" (i.e. work) and "holy activities" (i.e. prayer, spiritual life). Of course I am not going as far as some to state: "work is prayer/worship", but I am highlighting the fact that it is still the same "you" who works, who deals with others, who has a place in the world and society through your work. If work has little or no meaning for you, or even if it is seen as a burden, it is important to "work on" that issue because it is destructive, it doesn't create deep peace in you, and leads to a feeling of being unsettled, unsatisfied and frustrated. A significantly large part of your energy is involved, then, in something that is damaging you. Is this good? Can this contribute to a good and healthy Spiritual Life? Does this please God?

The situation is exacerbated by unemployment, for how then can we find fulfilment in some form of work, even be it voluntary work? How can we see God present during those daily eight or more hours? This is the challenge and one of the first steps that will help us to emerge from a lukewarm Spiritual Life.

Of prime importance in this light is Order. A disorganised person in daily life often creates a disorganised spiritual life. The goal is not to have random virtues, but to practise them in an organised way. One can have excellent virtues but if they are managed badly, great damage can result.

Thus the effort we make to create an image of ourselves for the world, to take our place in it, to grow, is of utmost importance. When the young rich man asked Jesus what he was supposed to do in order to gain Eternal Life, the Lord did not immediately reply to him: "come and follow me." No! He started by assessing the human foundations of the young man's Call, when he asked the latter whether he had fulfilled Moses' commandments? Let us for a moment consider the hypothesis that the answer was "no", and that this gentleman was not working, or better still, was not happy in his work life. Granted, nobody admits that "work" is always an enjoyable experience, free of stress, and effort! There is no reward without the necessary effort, although of course, one can adjust effort/energy, time, quality and outcome, to see if it is worth it, in order to employ most efficiently one's talents, capacity, expertise, and so on.

But here, in my humble view, within a serious and committed spiritual life, what matters is to focus on our work and a place where God is as well. Work is not an empty space where God is absent. God is not waiting for us outside of our Work-Space only. He is waiting for us during our work time. This is why doing high quality work is important. Negligence, random acts and careless behaviour in work cannot expect a good spiritual life to result.

Surprisingly enough, however, God pays attention to this. Just pause for a moment and think of it: you are the same person in the eyes of God when you pray and when you work. Can you deceive yourself? Can you fake it? Can you deceive God? Impossible! You are the same person, here, there and everywhere. You can't have a double standard: wanting God, wanting on the one hand a good Spiritual Life and have on the other an average quality or standard of work.

Let me take a very simple example: a few years ago I was teaching a young man a way of doing Lectio Divina based on the daily readings of the Mass. He said that he understood, and promised that he would start to practise it. I met him on a regular basis for a few months and checked on his practice of it. He said that he was doing it as I had explained it to him. I never ventured into asking for more details – in hindsight that was an error as we will see. A few years later both of us were involved in doing some cleaning. After having done his part, I asked him whether he had cleaned a particular area, to which he replied in the affirmative. By pure luck, I happened to be passing through the area he had cleaned and to my utter surprise it had not been done properly – or at least, with the thoroughness I had expected. I have to admit this was a big lesson in my life – not to rely on the simple reply: "yes I did it." I thought bitterly that his answer at odd times was always " yes, I have done it." So, I wondered, was his Lectio Divina done in the same way in which he had cleaned that area? This was deeply thought-provoking.

Let us return to the point about work: if you are good at certain things, and you have proved you can do them, then you are handed more important matters to deal with. The Kingdom of God is the most important thing in life, and it is not offered immediately but is preceded by a period of preparation. This is why the Lord himself says: 'Well done, good and faithful servant! You have been faithful with little things; I will put you in charge of greater things." (Matthew 25:21)

Of course you might be outraged by what I say, and you might extrapolate and apply what I am saying and deduce and conclude differently. But if we try humbly to apply that to ourselves, I am sure we can benefit and emerge from a lukewarm Spiritual Life. I would simply say: why do we expect the Lord to help us exit from a lukewarm lethargic Spiritual Life while we continue to be lukewarm in our work?

To the lay eye they seem unrelated, but I hope you might reconsider it and start to see that the very opposite is true.

God promised the Land to Abraham and swore to give it to him. But in fact, it took more than 400 years to realise this. First and foremost, God wanted Abraham's children to work, become active, commit to daily life and to their society, even if they were in a foreign land (Egypt), living amongst pagans (Egyptians)..; it is only then that He started to make things happen, and with his Arm, he saved them and brought them to a different land.

Let us now explore a question/objection here: can a Committed Spiritual Life help a disorganised person put some order in his or her life?

Let me reword that objection/question: can a Spiritual Life, i.e. a personal relationship with the Lord Jesus play a role in mending my life and getting back an ordered life, attentive to detail and conscientious at work? Of course yes, the Grace of God can help: we read about powerful conversions where a person who was leading a very bad life, came to discover the Lord and started by His Grace to change and become better, cleaner, more organised, committed in society and work.

Think of any big sinner (just for the sake of having a clear picture before us) who is struck by the Grace of God... led by it, arising from his mud, and starting to lead a good life. Think of the Prodigal son, who wasn't leading an orderly life, and still was struck by the Grace of God, came back to

112

himself, thought of his error, changed direction, prayed, asked for forgiveness and started his way back home. It must be said that one can re-start this way.

But the question I was addressing during my talk and the audience hearing it were different. They were Christians, whom, at a certain point in past years, had started to lead a committed christian life, a good Spiritual Life, but with the business of life they had got to a lukewarm point.

Think of the third soil of the Parable of the Sower: we are talking here about "good" Christians, who to a certain extent are committed, but still, the business and concerns of life have become so strong as to be compared to the spikes or thorns capable of suffocating the Word of God in them... so that they have reached a lukewarm state in their spiritual life.

To their utter surprise, I brought them back to consider their work place and not to investigate their Spiritual Life! Maybe Spiritual Life meant an escape to them? Maybe Work was lived as a dichotomy?

Let us remember that God is very present during our work time and sees how we work... In conclusion therefore, the message here is: the way we deal with work directly affects our Spiritual Life.

Please don't hesitate to have a look at the next chapter: The Duties of my State.

The Duties of my State

For some the teaching of the First Level Course will look as if it is focusing exclusively on the practice of Lectio Divina and the Prayer of the Heart (LD and PH). A further cause for concern may be that, initially, many may feel they do not have the time in their daily life to dedicate one hour to one and one hour or more to the other. People, being full of good will, can then become very frustrated and feel that they are failing God, by failing to implement two practices that seemed absolutely sound and stimulating in the course.

In the case of those who cannot initially find time (there might be many), I offer an important piece of advice and a "trick" to solve the problem. First it is important not to worry and not to panic because of the fact that one cannot find the time. Then I suggest that there is a powerful prayer we can say and if it is done with sincerity, an extremely powerful response on the Lord's part could be released, namely,

"Dear Lord, I see the importance of the daily practice of Lectio Divina and of the Prayer of the Heart,
but as you know I don't have time, but please find me the time,
reorganise my life in order to reach this goal."

In fact it is God's part to help us at this stage. Our part is to open our eyes to see how he will do it. In the meantime we do what we can, with five, ten or fifteen minutes found here and there.

But let us say that for a while God does not do anything, for the simple reason that our duties cannot change. A mother of young children remains a mother of young children, her situation will not change that much for a few years. She might then feel very frustrated, disappointed, and maybe depressed by the fact that, on one hand she really earnestly wants to take time for Jesus only, and on the other hand she cannot because of her daily duties as a wife and mother. Here I would like to indicate some important ways on how to manage this time of our life, until, some greater windows of time can open up. Ironically what I am about to say will seem opposed to what the teaching in the Course advises.

The element of the "duties of the state" (devoir d'état) is a fundamental element. It is a strong, clear, immovable manifestation of God's will for us.

The duties of the said wife and mother are clear and evident, but Jesus calling her to follow Him at this stage of her life should not overwhelm unnecessarily, for He knows what He is doing perfectly well. Therefore a positive outcome can be entertained, with the possibility of following Him in this context of lack of time for intimate prayer.

It is undeniable that the obstacle of the lack of time during the day looks insurmountable, and this reminds me of what St Therese says about the horse. Celine her sister (Sister Genevieve) tells the story in her book Conseils et Souvenirs:

"All discouraged, and with a heavy heart because of a combat that looked unsurmountable I came to see her saying: This time it is impossible, I can't rise above it!
– This doesn't surprise me, she replied. We are too little to put ourselves above the difficulties, we need to cross them from underneath.
She reminded me of something that happened to us in our youth. We were at Alençon at some friend's place; a horse was just in front of the entrance of the garden's gate preventing us from entering. while other persons were searching for another access, our little friend [Therese Lehoux, who was seven, the age of Celine] easily found the solution of passing underneath the horse. She went first, extended her hand to me; I followed her taking with me Therese and without bowing too much our small bodies we reached the goal.
She concluded by saying: this is what we gain when we make the effort to be small. There are no obstacles for the small ones, they sneak everywhere.
[...]" (*Conseils et Souvenirs*, Sr Genevieve)

What seems an obstacle to us is the duties of our state, the difficulty to find some spare time in order to dedicate it to Jesus (LD and PH). This is the "horse", standing in our way to Jesus in prayer. The good news is that if we are small, humble, accepting our place in life and our state, we can "sneak through" meaning we can find Jesus through the events of our day. Otherwise, we will not see through them, we will seek alternate means, and we will try to find a way in the midst of them, like the adults in the story, and we will get more and more frustrated, angry, and maybe in the end depressed, feeling that we have failed Jesus and that this is our fault. It can become a constant fight, generate great tension, and put our nerves on edge. Rather the focus should be on Jesus who entered into the life of this young mother and called her when she was married and with children. So this is the actual frame-work of His Call for her. He knows that and He is capable of renewing her within this framework. In his wisdom He knows what suits her and us best.

In the Spiritual Life we cannot separate "the moments of prayer" from the moments of "daily life". Why? During the moments of prayer we meet Jesus the individual, in an intimate way. He is the head of an immense body. The first people to pay attention to in this body are one's husband, and one's children i.e.: one's family, one's daily life. Then of course come neighbours, friends, more distant family... All these make up Jesus' Body. But Jesus is One, the Head, the one we want to meet in our personal prayer-time while we meet his Body during the rest of the day. Jesus is the one we love, and Jesus cannot be split into two, or simply "beheaded", with our keeping only the intimate Jesus and casting His Body aside. It is of utmost importance to find and love Jesus' Body according to the new way of loving He is teaching us, to be led by Him. It is important to attend to the detail of His Presence in His Body... the beauty of meeting Him in His Body... through His Body... of loving Him in His Body.

What did Our Lady do? She too, was a wife, and a mother. She had her house to manage, her family to take care of. Yet – after Jesus – she had the deepest possible spiritual life on earth. Seen from outside, she led a very simple life, similar to millions and millions of other women. But hers was totally, totally different....
The "framework" is the same... but she was able to dedicate time to all her duties as well as find God in all her spare moments and be with Him. Let us invite her into our homes to teach us. Otherwise our spiritual life can be seriously jeopardised.
Jesus is really present throughout the day. Attention and care given to Him during the day in the persons we meet, in the different circumstances of the day, are a fundamental Spiritual Experience. All things considered, maybe this was not mentioned enough in the opening course (Initiation into Spiritual Life). However, in my view I felt this this would unbalance the

course, because the said course not only encourages a full new attention to Christ, but it also provides the tools for achieving this. Admittedly I do not take "exceptions" into consideration.... Maybe one could say that "exceptions" are the norm for many busy persons who come to the course. Maybe so, but still, in my humble view, the contents of the course should first and foremost provide the tools – bearing in mind that the first level course is not everything, it is only the starting point. So the "lesson" of this post is a continuation of the above-mentioned course.

> Now,
> I am going to concentrate
> On my Duties.
>
> *They reveal to me God's Will.*
>
> The challenge is to fulfil them in a divine way.
>
> *Doing small things in a* Great *way.*

Taking all this into consideration, we can conclude that it is important to remember that if we have a huge desire to find Jesus and follow him, He Himself has a desire that is thousands of times greater to find us and grab hold of us. Let us then, in all simplicity, allow him to find us and to draw us close to him. Let us leave Jesus and not us, to be in control of our spiritual life. Let us trust Jesus, humbly, totally, unconditionally, let us trust the one who called us, the one who knows all the details of our day, and the one who is hidden within each of these details, "playing" hide and seek with us.

"Lord Holy Spirit open my eyes so I can see Jesus within each event of my day,

open my eyes so I can notice the immense richness of each moment of my day,

make me understand that there is no lost time during the day,

important moments and less important moments.

Teach me O Lord how to leave God for God[11].

Lord Jesus teaching me how to love at every moment of the day."

---

[11] "Leave God for God" is an expression used by St Vincent de Paul, explaining to his daughters that when a poor person knocks at their door while they are praying, they should leave God (in the chapel) for God (who is knocking at the door).

The Unavoidable Mystical Dimension of Christianity

Some people might argue that there is no "mystical dimension" in Christianity. Others would say that "there is one", but that it is "not for everybody". Others will claim: "we can't describe 'mystical'", so we remain in the dark or worse – with the feeling of ambiguity.

Let me start by **defining** what I mean here by "mystical dimension". In front of a phenomena that is very difficult to describe, where two (or more) beings are truly, but mysteriously (and strangely), united, or interwoven, no other word can be applied to it than "mystical". It is like saying: "hidden", "difficult to describe", or "ineffable".

Let me take two examples that will very easily help us get closer to this dimension in Christianity. Again, this dimension is so fundamental that if we empty Christianity of it, Christianity will no longer qualify as Christianity.

I- The first example I will take is Communion.

Two mystical acts were willingly performed by Jesus:
1- at one point in time, He took some bread and said: "this is my Body".
2- at another no less inexplicable point He said: "eat it", so "I can live in you and you in me" (John 6).

Lets face it:

1- A loaf of bread is not a human being. Not even a divine Being.

2- Eating a human (or divine) Being is a very strange act. How would you do it? What would happen if you did it?

This is what I call "mystical": it is something very real, but is difficult to grasp. And it is still very **dynamic**, **active** and **transformative**. Jesus says that the human being, in order to be complete, requires more, needs to be **grafted** onto another larger being: Jesus. When Paul of Tarsus says: *"it is not me who lives, but Christ who lives in me"*, he embodies in this expression the very essence of the mystical aspect of Christianity. You'll certainly agree with me, that this is not just "a secondary aspect" in Christianity. It touches its essence. It is not an optional aspect.

The contact that God wants to make with us is not an intellectual or notional contact. It is a **deep**, **real**, **transformative** contact. First God becomes a human being and takes on a human nature (without changing His Divine Nature). Secondly, He wants us to be united to Him and **transform**ed in Him. On the Cross He will unite Himself with each one of us. This will be performed by the mysterious (mystical) Action of the Holy Spirit, the Master of anything Mystical.

II- Let us take a second example, that precedes "Communion" and is at its core: Baptism. Baptism says St. Paul is to be immersed in Christ, it is to **participate** to His Death, and therefore **experience** the transformative Power of His Resurrection. Baptism is a Seed, Jesus in us, who will grow in us – the new being in us, or "the new man". This Divine Seed, planted in us, needs to grow until it reaches its fullness. All this is "mystical". It is difficult to grasp. **Real**, **indispensable**, **unavoidable**. It allows us to get so close to Jesus, to get united to Him. And yet even though we struggle to escape from it, we are unable to define it.

How would you describe this necessary union between Christ and us, a union that does not generate confusion, that far from endangering our freedom actually fosters it, as a union that directly impacts on us?

To put it in a nutshell: just ask any fervent Catholic or Orthodox faithful to describe to you what he or she feels right after Communion, right after having received the Body and Blood of Jesus. They will unanimously agree that this very moment is the **highest point** of the day or the week. That it is indeed **a deeply intense moment**. The moment when they are **the closest to Jesus, to God**. The moment when they feel that their prayer has been answered. They often feel peace. They would like this moment to last. I would simply call this moment: a simple, daily or weekly, **mystical moment**. Real, but difficult to describe. It happens in the deepest part of ourselves, but it remains hidden from our consciousness. Even so, a great peace and stillness "seeps" through to our consciousness. Some real change in our external being does happen if we allow it.

With this we have arrived at the essence of Christianity, at **the unbreakable nucleus that constitutes Christianity**. Christianity is indeed "**mystical" in its essence**. So please, let us not hide from this dimension, let us acknowledge it. God, in Christianity is not a remote Being in whom one believes or not. No. He is not a set of Dogmas. He is a Being. United with Him we are more complete. Just try Him.

How would you describe the way we are united with him? The answer would indubitably be: "Mystically". We are united to Him mystically deep within us – you cannot really grasp it directly – but we are in truth united with Him. He is truly in us, and with us. *"dwell in Me"* says Jesus. *"without me you can't do anything"* (John 15). Quite a statement. It is a mystical statement that shows **the mystical dimension of our entire day**.

Here is a mystical Prayer:

> **Soul of Christ**, sanctify me.
> **Body of Christ**, save me.
> **Blood of Christ**, inebriate me.
> **Water from the side of Christ**, wash me. **Passion of Christ**, strengthen me.
> **O good Jesus**, hear me.
> **Within your wounds**, hide me.
> Never let me be separated from **You.**
> From the malignant enemy, defend me. At the hour of death, call me; and bid me come to **You.** That with your saints I may praise **You** forever and ever. Amen. **(St. Ignatius Loyola)**

Lets Face "Mystical"

In John Chapter 6, when Jesus starts to say that He is "the Bread" and that that Bread is his own flesh (not "body" but "flesh") and his own blood, people were shocked. And the good thing is that John, the Apostle, is underlining the fact that people were shocked. John is not avoiding the difficulty inherent in the "mystical dimension" that Jesus is offering: eating his flesh and drinking his blood.

"- Too close!" "- Too intimate!" is what people manage to say at best. John gives us the spontaneous reaction of some people: "How can this man give us (his) flesh to eat?"

Did Jesus let the subject drop? On the contrary John does not seem to imply that. Did Jesus say to himself: "ok, this is too difficult for them, I will then stop speaking about this difficult topic, let's change the subject", or "let us dilute it a bit and make it milder"? No, He didn't. Seriously, we should be surprised by the fact that Jesus kept going on.

He just simply continued on His track. He even emphasised the difficulty, and, to a degree, He made it more difficult. He tried to explain, develop, expand:

"Amen, amen, I say to you, unless you eat the flesh of the Son of Man and drink his blood, you do not have life within you. Whoever eats my flesh and drinks my blood has eternal life, and I will raise him on the last day. For my flesh is true food, and my blood is true drink. Whoever eats my flesh and drinks my blood remains in me and I in him." (John 6) Later, in that same text of John 6, John will say that, at this juncture, some stopped following Jesus.

Facing the "Mystical Dimension" of our own Faith

At some point each Christian has to face the "mystical dimension" of his/her faith, responsibly, as an adult, and decide which side he/she wants to take. To enter deeply into this mystical dimension, or just drop his Christian faith. Jesus, assuredly, will not change his plan just because "we don't like it", or "we have some difficulty grasping it". He is ever ready to help, however, if we are opened to Him, if we ask for His help. But He will not bypass the "mystical" dimension.

– What, then, is mystical? – "Mystical" can be surprisingly confusing. But it is real and is deeply embedded in the core of becoming a Christian. When Jesus invites us to "eat his Flesh" (John 6), to "dwell in Him" (John 15), when St. Paul says: "it is not me who lives but Jesus who lives in me", we are simply in the "mystical" dimension.

We inhabit the three-dimensional world space: 3D. We can add "time" as a fourth dimension. I do not want to add more dimensions and turn this into a mathematical marathon, but just want to point out the everyday human being that grasping the existence of four dimensions is easy. Hence, 2D comprises looking at a simple photograph. With 3D and if it moves we have we have 3D + time (motion).

The "mystical dimension" is one more dimension that is totally necessary for Christian life.

In order to understand the "mystical dimension", let me use an analogy, just to open the way to this "new dimension".
Have you ever watched an episode of "Drop Dead Diva"? It is the story of a twenty-four-year-old girl, **Deb**, who is an aspiring model (you can imagine her figure), who has a car accident, reaches heaven, and then comes back to earth but in the bigger body of a thirty-two-year-old girl, **Jane**, who is a lawyer, and has who just died. The soul (and spirit) of one person, Deb, has fallen into the body (and the brain) of another person: Jane.

Note: Of course, I am not at all going to address the issue of "is this possible or not". For Christianity it is simply not acceptable, for one body is designated for one soul only; numerically speaking a particular body body is designated for a particular soul, in a unique and definitive way. I am just taking this TV series case as an analogy. Many people accept this "mystical" game, even if it is not possible to have it in real life, so I just hope it may help us to get closer to the daily Christian "mystical dimension".

"Transformed", not "lost"

When Paul says: **"I no longer live, but Christ lives in me"** (Gal 2:20), of course it is not at all identical to Jane's case in "Drop Dead Diva", but it is remotely similar and opens the way to what is more meaningful. When Jesus grows in us, and becomes more alive (remember the "Spiritual Marriage" or "union with Jesus-God" we saw previously), we still have all our being (our soul is not lost or replaced by Jesus' one like in Jane's case). We still have our body, our soul, and our spirit. We don't lose any part of our being. Our being is renewed, purified, elevated. We have merely been "inserted" and "rooted" in the humanity of Jesus but not lost. We have been "Improved" but not lost.

Our body **is in** Jesus' body, our soul, **is in** Jesus' soul, our spirit **is in** Jesus' spirit. Our entire human nature (body, soul and spirit) is in His human nature. Similarly, our entire human nature – dwelling in His human nature – is united to his divinity. Remember that His human Nature is united to the Divine Nature of the Second Person of the Divine Trinity. The diagram below will helps us visualise the "new life" in Jesus.

The "human being" – each one of us – on the right is invited to enter into the humanity of Jesus (on the left). In fact, St Augustine about Communion says that we think we eat Him, but in fact He eats us. The three arrows in the diagram show us that our body enters (is rooted) into his Body as are the soul and the spirit.

The word "enters" is, on reflection, a rather weak term to describe what is really happening, that is we are being **transformed** in Him. Transformation, again, doesn't mean we lose our humanity, our body, our soul, our spirit. They are enriched, with Christ growing and increasingly taking over the "space within us as He moves and acts through us. We do not lose our will for it is being transformed in His.

St. Thérèse of the Child Jesus says that when she does good things to her sisters, it is in fact Jesus acting in her who is doing these things. She does not mean that her personality has been undermined, but that Jesus is alive in her and moves her in a higher an newer way : she doesn't lose her will, her freedom.

As you can notice on the diagram, Jesus' humanity (the square that includes His body, soul and spirit) is placed in the Divine Person of the Logos (the large rectangle), the Second Person of the Trinity, and is united to it.

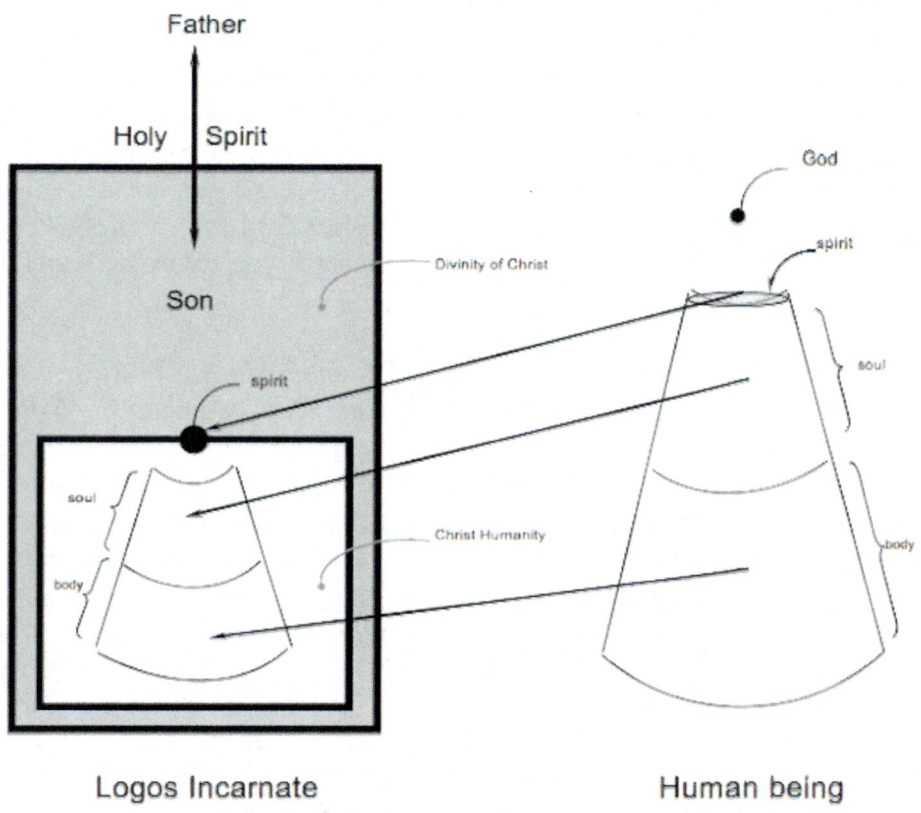

It is like as if a plant is uprooted – "our humanity" (body, soul and spirit) – and is then re-rooted in the Person of Jesus – the Logos Incarnate. Being rooted in Jesus is tantamount to acquiring a mystical person.

The Mystical Dimension of the New Commandment

"One of the scribes came to Jesus and asked him, «Which is the first of all the commandments?» [L; SEP] *Jesus replied, "The first is this: 'Hear, O Israel!*

The Lord our God is Lord alone! [SEP] *You shall love the Lord your God with all your heart, with all your soul, with all your mind, and with all your strength.'* [SEP] *The second is this: 'You shall love your neighbour as yourself.' There is no other commandment greater than these."* [SEP] *The scribe said to him, "Well said, teacher. You are right in saying, 'He is One and there is no other than he.'* [SEP] *And 'to love him with all your heart, with all your understanding, with all your strength, and to love your neighbour as yourself' is worth more than all burnt offerings and sacrifices."* [SEP] *And when Jesus saw that he answered with understanding, he said to him,* **"You are not far from the kingdom of God."** *And no one dared to ask him any more questions."* (Mk 12:28-34)

One could say that as a statement, « *you are not far from the Kingdom of God* » is rather disappointing, for Jesus did not say: "you are **in** the Kingdom of God".

Nobody can question the validity of the two Commandments of Moses; they are not abrogated by Jesus: "Do not think that I have come to abolish the law or the prophets" (Mt 5:17). However, at the same time there is a clear difference between the Law of Moses and the 'Law" of Jesus. Certainly, there is no contradiction between them, but there is a superiority, a perfection in Jesus' Commandment: *"I have come [...] to fulfil [the commandments]"* (Mt 5:17). When Jesus shows the way to the Kingdom to the rich young man, He starts by checking if he has fulfilled Moses' Commandments, when He says: *"did you fulfil the Commandments?"* to which the young man replies: *"yes, from my youth"*. Jesus here is speaking about Moses' Commandments, summarised by the two commandments mentioned above. In this case, as mentioned above, Jesus does not say either: *"you are in the Kingdom"* but He reiterates the statement: still *"you lack one thing"* (Mc 10:21) in order to enter the Kingdom. St. John says that Jesus' Commandment is not new, but it is new "in us" (1John 2:7-8): *"Beloved, I am writing you no new commandment, but an old commandment that you have had from the beginning; the old commandment is the word that you have heard. 8 Yet I am writing you* **a new commandment that is true** *in him and* **in you**, *because the darkness is passing away and the true light is already shining."* (1John 2:7-8)

The question now is to try to understand in what lies the newness of the "new Commandment" and how it is "superior", "more perfect" than the two Commandments.

"I give you a new Commandment, that you love one another; just as I have loved you, you also should love one another." (John 13:41) Jesus is very clear: *"unless your righteousness exceeds that of the scribes and Pharisees, you will never enter the kingdom of heaven."* (Mt 5:20) The mystical dimension of our transformation in Jesus, makes Jesus grow, live in us, and act in us and with us: *"it is no longer I who live, but Christ lives in me"* (Ga 2:20). This is why it is not possible to just "apply" the New Commandment, without being transformed in Jesus, in order to "enter the Kingdom". This is why St. John in his first letter says that the Commandment is "new in us". St. John states it very well: *"the darkness [in you] is passing away and the true Light [Jesus] is already shining [in you]."* (1John 2:7-8)

Without the mystical dimension, that implies real transformation of our being, letting the "new man" in us grow (Jesus in us), **there is no Christianity**.

The Mystical Instinct

Introduction

I would like now to speak about the mystical dimension, but as an instinct. I am not alluding to the natural instinct or desire that every human being has to seek God, the divine, but the supernatural desire, i.e. the desire that is the result of a Call from Jesus and a Grace given by God to a specific person, at a specific time in his or her life, and done in a specific way. This, as will be seen, is not an innate instinct but a new grafted instinct that will pervade the very depths of our being and permeate our very lives. St. Paul endorses this when he invites us to be led by the Holy Spirit (Gal 5:25; Romans 8:14). He goes on to mention that in the new spiritual life thus engendered and given by Jesus, there are at the core of our being (our heart) impulses or movements generated by the Holy Spirit. These are akin to a new supernatural instinct grafted onto us. In addition to this, I would like to explore the "instinctual" aspect of it. Do we become like robots? Does being led, moved by the Holy Spirit, turn us into spiritual "puppets". How is our freedom affected? In which sense would we call it "instinct"?

Important Note: The subject of this chapter is very rich and covers a great variety of connected subjects. Therefore, herein, whenever it is needed, I will allude to previous posts in order to offer the reader every possibility to deepen the subject of his choice.

What is the meaning of "mystical"?

"Mystical" means hidden. By extension it has been applied to all the manifestations of a developed spiritual life, which in turn implies direct connection with God, visions and supernatural phenomena. Very often it is viewed essentially as being closely linked to the discovery and exploration of God's world, its graces and growth of intimacy with God. With this in mind we should distinguish clearly between what is the core of mysticism, open to everyone, and what is not the core (levitation, stigmata, physical visions,…), given only to some. In order, then, to understand the difference between peripheral phenomena (mystical phenomena) and the core reality, and in order to learn discernment for this please see below. St Therese of the Child Jesus who is the perfect embodiment of a supremely mystical life (a spiritual life) that gives no evidence of any extraordinary and peripheral graces.

Is it a natural instinct or a spiritual gift?
St. John of the Cross states that the human being desires God in two ways: naturally and supernaturally, i.e. under the influence of a grace given by God. What interests us is the latter because it is this grace that is invited to grow and to help us reach Union with Christ.[12]

What is the "mystical instinct"?
How can the "mystical instinct" be defined? Going back to the Fathers of the Church we find that they developed a spiritual doctrine stating that once the spiritual journey is embarked upon, under the action of the Holy Spirit, inner spiritual senses do develop in us; new capacities/senses that are spiritual are gifted to us – pure effects of the grace of God – developing in us a new range of senses that will allow us to find our bearings in God's world. We can then see God, hear Him, etc… If for the sake of an entirely theoretical explanation, we unite these new senses, blending them together, we can say that this amalgam resembles a new theological "instinct" that guides us toward God, helps us to sense Him, follow Him and serve Him – and thereby allows the new man in us to grow. It goes without saying that these senses, and this instinct, are directly fed by the Theological Virtues of Faith, Hope and Love. These three alone connect us directly to God. This instinct, it must be remembered, has been given to us in a seminal form during baptism, and it is the work of the Holy Spirit which, together with our collaboration, causes it to grow. This goes to show that the mystical instinct is far from being a purely animalistic instinct, but proves rather that the new organism, embodying this new sense, is now developing. From this we can now imply that it undergoes different phases of growth. Furthermore, this mystical quality – through the action of the theological acts – connects us with God who has been leading us in the first place. It can be compared to the inter-connection of the eyes, hands, feet, heart and will. With the ensuing growth, the more the new man has the upper hand, the more the Holy Spirit's impulses are sensed (see Romans 8).

---

[12] see in the coming books the chapter: The Sacred Threshold of the Kingdom".

Is being guided by our "mystical instinct" going against reason?

Going against reason is never the case. St. John of the Cross in fact emphatically states: come to terms with reason, common sense should guide us as well in deep spiritual life. But, it must be avowed that the mystical instinct is sometimes beyond reason: it comes from God and goes back to Him. However, the solid base to which we must paradoxically often return is reason. The grace of God will often help us fulfil our daily duties. Is that against reason? No, on the contrary. We are all subject to the universal time-frame of seven days per week and twenty-four hours per day, with no additions possible… our day is universally ordered into times for sleeping, eating, resting, entertainment, prayer, work,… Providentially, rather, this new instinct, with its attendant graces, will help us, exteriorly, to do the same things, but in a vastly improved manner, with greater attention to quality and detail. What is noteworthy here, is that the difference lies in the fact that this instinct will guide us from within to do everything in a completely different way, a way that is connected to God. What, then, can totally attract us with such magnetism to God? Only the Mystical Instinct. Will it force us to act against reason? No, on the contrary, it will move us from within to connect directly with God while we are apparently undertaking our normal routines. The difference lies in the deeper inner world.

Can any human being have it?

Yes, providing he or she has been through a conversion, and spiritual growth has commenced.

Is there a call for a mystical life?

Yes there definitely is. We are all called to follow Jesus. And this journey is by definition "mystical". Please see the chapter: Is mysticism for everybody in the book "The Foundations of Spiritual Life According to St. Teresa of Avila" The unavoidable mystical dimension of Christianity (see above). The Mystical Dimension of the New Commandment (see above).

Can it be triggered?

Jesus' words "I called you, not you called me" (John 15:16) clearly indicate that the initial move is made by God. However, much depends on us[13]. Here

---

[13] See the coming books on Prayer of the Heart, "What Depends on Us".

is what depends on God.[14] A more detailed theological explanation of the difference between "general help" and "particular help" with St. Thomas Aquinas can be found in the *Summa Teologica* I-IIae Q. 109, A.6.

Can spiritual growth be further developed ?
It most emphatically can: this new instinct is constantly refined, by the addition of a developing and in-depth discernment. It is to be remembered that God is Spirit and cannot be deceived. We can only learn to discover Him... He is our sole teacher. (See below): The importance of leading a Spiritual Life.[15]

Can it be hindered?
Of course it can. Ignorance, is one of the main reasons for hindering growth. Spiritual laziness only exacerbates this.

Can one develop it more than others?
Most definitely, as holiness has grades and levels; in fact we could say, with St. Therese, to Jesus: "I want it all, I don't want half measures."

Are some temperaments more prone to it?
We all are invited to have a share in it. (see 1 Timothy 2:4 and John 15:15)

Can it be faked?
Unfortunately, deviations are possible. The Devil can easily interfere, and the Lord allows this in order to test our obedience to Him. Charlatans exist as well, in the name of religion.

Can it be dangerous?
Anything in the spiritual life not led by discernment (through spiritual direction) can lead to real disaster.

---

[14] See in the book ""The Foundations of Spiritual Life According to St. Teresa of Avila" the chapter: "The Particular Help of the Grace of God in St Teresa of Avila".

[15] Other important notion will be presented in a coming book: "Ensuring Steady Growth". In the book mentioned in the previous note one can find the chapter on Mapping Spiritual Life. Also the book: "The Spiritual Journey", by Jean Khoury.

Is the mystical instinct the same as the contemplative instinct?

Some people would consider themselves more contemplatives, and others more active. These distinctions tend to be misleading. Although we cannot deny that some human dispositions are more contemplative, introvert, and others are more active, extrovert, we cannot completely dismiss the contemplative (mystical instinct) dimension in extroverts and the active dimension of spiritual life in introverts. Balance, and communication between the two dimensions is valid for all – the rest encompasses only grades of intensity.

How can I know if I am called to it?

Being personally and directly called to it does differ from the general theoretical statement: all are called to it[16].

How can we understand the "instinctual" aspect of it?

"Instinct" means an almost uncontrollable way of thinking or acting – a more spontaneous way of acting. Providing this spiritual instinct grows in us, and grows properly, in the correct direction… we can say that this is the result of God's new life in us: the Holy Spirit dwelling in us.

Do we become like robots?

Is being led, moved by the Holy Spirit, turning us into a species of spiritual puppet? What happens to our freedom? Of course not. The example of dancing (think of a waltz) sheds an interesting light on the relationship between our free will and God's impulses. When learning to dance it can sometimes take years of exercise for a learner to master this art. Does dancing require only one of the partners? No, it requires both. Does dancing mean that the lady leads? No, this is not the case. Paradoxically, when you see both dancing you have the impression that the lady is as light as a feather, and that she is following all the hand and body movements of the gentleman, like a puppet. But is she a puppet? Quite the contrary, for over the years of learning she has been deeply transformed. The same applies to us: do we become the robots of the Grace of God? What happens to our free will? The

---

[16] Please see the chapter above: "A Call is a Call".

answer lies here: hours and hours of exercise, becoming connected, docile, in harmony with the Divine Partner.

In which sense would we call it "instinct"?
In the sense that this long friendship has seen the development of these virtues to the point that they now seem instinctual rather than painful and implying effort.

How does it relate to fervour?
The more we grow spiritually, the more this instinct grows. But there are phases of growth which follow the normal curve of holiness[17].

How does it relate to spiritual emulation?
Spiritual emulation as well as "mystical instinct'" is the result of a fervent spiritual life[18].

Will the "mystical instinct" differentiate us from the rest of the crowd?
The Mystic within us sees his "mystical instinct" grow, become surer, more discerning. But in the final analysis, as above-mentioned, it does not go against reason, for it comprises an inner instinct to seek out and connect with God all the time, to keep the Fire of His Love alive in us. Therefore, paradoxically, the "mystical instinct" make us more respectful of the authorities, and allows us at the same time to seemingly blend in with the crowd. If we follow this instinct we will do great things, as Jesus said. Without Jesus we are powerless (see John 15). This instinct, by drawing us closer to Him, will keep us connected with Jesus. And if by any chance we go astray, it will bring us back, with even greater humility.

---

[17] See the complete journey of growth in the book mentioned above: "The Spiritual Journey" by Jean Khoury.
[18] See the coming book on Spiritual Formation and its importance.

The Immersion in the Trinity

The very Palpable Trinity

Don't you think that we often look at the Trinity as an abstract distant "object"? Strangely, in the early Church, the Trinity was a reality Christians were immersed IN all the time. The Trinity was very palpable, lived, tasted: an experience. How did this happen?

"Immersed", according to the dictionary, is "to be covered completely in a liquid".

The liquid can cover you, but it can sometimes penetrate your skin as well, like oil, no?

Once it penetrates your being, e.g. chemicals, you might be transformed into something like it, no?

Baptism was performed (and is still done in various Churches) by a triple immersion: one had to be immersed a first time: "in the name of the Father", a second time "in the Son", and a third time "in the Holy Spirit", one God. The Greek meaning of the word "baptised" actually means "being immersed" and further endorses this method.

Baptism, then, is not about being immersed and then emerging from the water once and for all. It is meant to be a constant spiritual state of immersion, in which one remains baptised (immersed) all one's life.

St. Paul greets his fellow Christians in Corinth this way: *"The grace of the Lord **Jesus Christ**, and the love of **God**, and the communion of the **Holy Spirit**, be with you all. Amen."* (2 Co 13:13) He mentions Jesus first: because Jesus is the one sent by the Father to reveal the Trinity to us, to open out the Trinity for us; He is the entrance Gate to the Trinity. This is stressed when Matthew mentions the Father, followed by the Holy Spirit. This is a very genuine primitive order and is, indeed, kept by Matthew in his stunning presentation of the triple Immersion (Mt. 5 through to 7), namely, the teachings on the Son (Mt. 5), on the Father (Mt. 6), and on the Holy Spirit (Mt. 7), which, in addition and most significantly of all, are **one** teaching and not three.

To baptise somebody is to introduce the person INTO the life of the Trinity, to immerse him or her and to hand over to them the **responsibility** of remaining immersed. This depends on us. The teaching on how to remain immersed in each Person of the Trinity is presented by Matthew in his Gospel in the Sermon on the Mount right after the Beatitudes:

At the end of St. Matthew's Gospel, as the quotation below will illustrate, Jesus emphasises this keynote of the sacrament of Baptism when He asks his Apostles to do as follows: to help new Christians **remain** immersed in each one of the Persons of the Trinity. In order to do so his teaching is all one and triune.

It is our responsibility to put into practice the teaching of each immersion, in order to REMAIN immersed. *"Dwell in me"* says Jesus in John 15, or in other words: "Dwell in the Trinity", Dwell in the Son (by putting into practice Mt. 5) Dwell in the Father (by putting into practice Mt. 6) Dwell in the Holy Spirit by putting into practice Mt 7).

The end of Matthew's Gospel and his three chapters 5 to 7, in this manner, become one of the very first forms of Spiritual Theology…: teaching people how to dwell in the Trinity, how to dwell in each of the Persons of the

Trinity. This is Baptism as is summed up by Matthew at the end of his Gospel, with all its implications concerning the Trinity:

"Then Jesus approached and said to them, "All power in heaven and on earth has been given to me. SEP *Go, therefore, and make disciples of all nations,* **baptising (immersing)** *them in the name of the Father, and of the Son, and of the Holy Spirit,* SEP ***teaching*** *them to observe all that I have commanded you. And behold, I am with you always, until the end of the age."* (end of Mt, and is as well the summary of Mt 5-7)

It is of the **utmost importance,** then, not to forget that "baptising" and "teaching to observe" are in fact **one thing**, and that they mirror each other.

One last thing

A very early tradition, found in St Irenaeus (130-202), says that the Hands of the Father are the Son and the Holy Spirit. (St Irenaeus is the disciple of the disciple of St John the Evangelist.) Now, imagine the Father holding you, as a little baby with His Hands (the Son, and the Holy Spirit), immersing you, and always holding you.

This is one of the early spiritual ways of being for Christians. This is the earliest form of catechesis and is very practical. First comes the understanding that God has two Hands – the Son, and the Holy Spirit – and that He holds us with them. Our aim then should be never to escape from His Hands. Finally, as each hand has 5 fingers, in order to remain in the

137

Hands of the Father, we need to put into practice the 5 + 5 commandments we find in the Sermon on the Mount. The Son's 5 commandments are to be found in the second part of Mt. 5, and the 5 of the Holy Spirit in the five sections of Mt. 7. We need to learn once again how to count on the fingers of each hand: 1, 2, 3,…5, then again: 1, 2, 3…5. In this way, the Father can hold us, we are facing Him, and we can live the 7 sections of Mt. 6, dedicated to the Father and actually containing in it the "Our Father". Counting, remembering, putting into practice, will allow us to remain in the Hands of the Father, all the time, Face to face with Him.

So, when we say the Our Father, we say it in the position shown above. The Father is holding us – his little children – with His First Hand: the Son, and with His Second Hand: the Holy Spirit. We are Face to face.
Hope that helps not only your neurones but your "taste buds" as well. Let us taste the Trinity: get your swimming trunks (Mt. 5-7) and jump into the Triune Well.

Note: "Dogmata" for the Greek Philosophers was like advice, a great piece of wisdom to be put into practice, a short sentence, to reflect and ponder on, put into practice until it becomes part of us. The three dogmata (the Son, the Father and the Holy Spirit) are indeed to be put into practice, by living Mt. 5, 6 and 7.

The Importance of Leading a Spiritual Life

The mission of the School of Mary is to teach Spiritual Life to adults giving them the minimum necessary knowledge in order to have a personal spiritual life and allow our personal relationship with the Lord to grow and reach its fullness.

Teaching plays a very important part in allowing a healthy spiritual life to initiate and empower every person. Without that teaching, one remains ignorant of many vital and practical elements of our faith and therefore, unconsciously, is subject to random results in what one is doing in order to get closer to God. The reception of Grace, even with a sacramental life, can remain very limited, or even be obstructed.

Ignorance is sadly a key factor in this. Why? Because the person is not yet in control of his or her own personal spiritual life. Things are done randomly, just as they come, in an amateurish way. The consequences of this is an "under-life", a limited life, an under-developed life. Even if the person has some success in their family life or work, deep inside the core is lacking. His or her Christian life cannot blossom with only the commitment of an hour every week at Mass.

Mount of Beatitudes Church

Without teaching, therefore, there is no awareness. Without teaching one cannot properly handle one's spiritual responsibilities. However, we are talking here about a teaching that has practical implications, not just mere theory. The practical teaching shows us how to do something, which if we put it into practice will help us receive new graces. Consequently, our spiritual life blossoms like a flower in Spring. On the other hand, if we do not receive practical teaching, we will not know what God wants us to realise in our life: the gifts He wants to give us because we have not learned how to receive his grace in a fruitful way. Practical knowledge is vital because it reveals our identity and shows us what we are to do. It is of the utmost importance to know how to react when God moves us. He needs our cooperation. Amazingly, He will not force Himself on us and we need to have this awareness of how to receive his grace.

Teaching Dogma, Liturgy and Sacraments, teaching Moral Theology is good, but it will never work without a proper spiritual life, and without a practical teaching that facilitates it. The Catechism tells us this. Pope Benedict XVI tells us this in his first encyclical, *Deus Caritas Est* (*God is Love*). This is not new!

'Great is the mystery of the faith!'. The Church professes this mystery in the Apostles' Creed (Part One) and celebrates it in the sacramental liturgy (Part Two), so that the life of the faithful may be conformed to Christ in the Holy Spirit to the glory of God the Father (Part Three). This mystery, then, requires that the faithful believe in it, that they celebrate it, and that they live from it in a vital and personal relationship with the living and true God. This relationship is prayer. (CCC 2558)

But receiving a new Teaching, new to you, if not new in itself, pushes you out of your actual boundaries, out of your comfort zone. Who likes this? Very few people like the experience unless it is for a good reason. Even so, one can find it too assertive. One was living in a blissful state of ignorance but now the sudden arrival of this teaching on spiritual life upsets it! However, one has the opportunity now to control one's spiritual life; one can feel more responsibility for one's own life and the future, the spiritual future. It is also true, that the more you know, the more you receive, the more God will ask you later to give an account of concerning what you have received. However, God is just. He will not ask you to give what you do not have, or work on talents or gifts that you do not have or of what you are not aware.

But now that you start to discover the richness of the Gift of God, you can explore at the same time all that is needed to correspond to His Gift and receive the Graces God wants to give you – ironically, now you have more work to do. You need to move on from the lethargic state in which you were, to a more pro-active state. Staying still now will mean one is rooted in Jesus through silent prayer. Wouldn't we want to remain rooted in Jesus in everything? To our advantage, what is happening is that a deep spiritual life is being offered to allow us to remain centred, grounded and rooted in God. The result is a great sense of peace and contentment. Curiously, the majority of human beings do not find it, or have it, so they remain agitated, wandering here and there without a goal. Isn't it preferable to maintain a core of stillness, of quiet, in your busy life?

This requires effort and is indeed demanding. This is why, many years ago toward the end of one of my courses, while teaching, a gentleman, attending the same First Level Course of Initiation into Spiritual Life (also called, "Solid Foundations") said to me in front of everybody: "Jean, why are you teaching us all this? Why are you giving us all this information about Spiritual Life?"

I thought he knew! And he did know! But his question in fact was saying between the lines: our lives will now have to bear more responsibility. Do we like this? Oh, that state of blissful ignorance, how we miss it! Yes, if God created us without our consent, He will not save us without our consent! (pro-active consent, active collaboration). As a consequence of this Teaching, things are becoming more complex, we ourselves need to move and do things! We need to learn more, practise, read!!

The other day, while teaching the *Solid Foundations* a lady said to me: "what happens if people don't know all these things? Can they still receive the Graces God wants to give them? What will happen to them?"

Hmm… I replied: "The aim of this Course is to take the student from a 'random' life in the Grace of God to a 'responsible' life". "Random" to "Responsible"! St. Paul says in his letter to the Romans:

"But how are men to call upon Him in whom they have not believed?

141

And how are they to believe in him of whom they have never heard? And how are they to hear without a preacher?" (Romans 10:14)

How will they know if they have not heard the Good News? This is why the Lord commands us to Evangelise, to Preach, to Teach, to "Form Disciples" for Him. It is not a choice; it is an order: go and preach the Good News! Spiritual Life is vital. Feeding your children is vital, it is not optional.

One of the greatest truths taught to us by Pope St. John Paul II is that every baptised person, by virtue of his or her Baptism, is a missionary. You can see this in his Encyclical letter *Redemptoris Missio*. It is by virtue of Baptism that we receive the *mandatum* (order), the "sending in mission". Let us remember as well that the Priest at the end of the Mass when he says, "Go in peace", is not saying: "…that's it, the Mass is ended, go back to your normal life". On the contrary, he is saying: "Now that you have received Christ in your heart, in your mind, in your will, in your emotions and in your imagination, I (as your Parish Priest, and in His name) am reminding you that now you have a Mission from Christ – to transmit Him to others, starting with your family, your neighbours and your workplace!

In sum, people cannot know what God wants to give them on a daily basis – "Give us our daily Bread" – if nobody explains it to them. There is a "Body of Teaching" dedicated to that: the science of knowing what God wants to give us (God's Gift) and how we can receive it on a daily basis. If nobody specialises in this Science, if nobody teaches this, we end up by having empty teaching, inedible bread, and our life becomes stagnant. If nobody teaches me, how will I know? If I do not know, I will not be able to do anything. I might receive a strong grace from time to time, like once a year during a Retreat, but nothing else! Instead of receiving "grace upon grace" (John 1), discovering the richness of the Gift of God, diving into its immensity, discovering the Love of Jesus and how it fills all dimensions of life, I will not be able to know Jesus, to fall in love with Him, to receive his "Daily Bread". I will be an "under-developed Christian…. In all honesty, would anyone consciously make a choice like this?

The Universal Call To Holiness In The Church

Catechism of the Catholic Church

PART THREE: LIFE IN CHRIST
 SECTION ONE MAN'S VOCATION LIFE IN THE SPIRIT
  CHAPTER THREE GOD'S SALVATION: LAW AND GRACE
   Article 2 GRACE AND JUSTIFICATION

IV. Christian Holiness

2012 "We know that in everything God works for good with those who love him . . . For those whom he fore knew he also predestined to be conformed to the image of his Son, in order that he might be the first-born among many brethren. and those whom he predestined he also called; and those whom he called he also justified; and those whom he justified he also glorified."[19]

2013 "All Christians in any state or walk of life are called to the fullness of Christian life and to the perfection of charity."[20] All are called to holiness: "Be perfect, as your heavenly Father is perfect."[21]
In order to reach this perfection, the faithful should use the strength dealt out to them by Christ's gift, so that . . . doing the will of the Father in everything, they may wholeheartedly devote themselves to the glory of God and to the service of their neighbour. Thus, the holiness of the People of God will grow in fruitful abundance, as is clearly shown in the history of the Church through the lives of so many saints.[22]

2014 Spiritual progress tends toward ever more intimate union with Christ. This union is called "mystical" because it participates in the mystery of Christ through the sacraments – "the holy mysteries" – and, in him, in the mystery of the Holy Trinity. God calls us all to this intimate union with him, even if the special graces or extraordinary signs of this mystical life are

---

[19] ⇒ Rom 8:28-30.
[20] LG 40 # 2. (see below the whole chapter)
[21] ⇒ Mt 5:48.
[22] LG 40 # 2. (see below the whole chapter)

granted only to some for the sake of manifesting the gratuitous gift given to all.

2015 The way of perfection passes by way of the Cross. There is no holiness without renunciation and spiritual battle.[23] Spiritual progress entails the ascesis and mortification that gradually lead to living in the peace and joy of the Beatitudes: *He who climbs never stops going from beginning to beginning, through beginnings that have no end. He never stops desiring what he already knows.*[24]

2016 The children of our holy mother the Church rightly hope for the grace of final perseverance and the recompense of God their Father for the good works accomplished with his grace in communion with Jesus.[25] Keeping the same rule of life, believers share the "blessed hope" of those whom the divine mercy gathers into the "holy city, the new Jerusalem, coming down out of heaven from God, prepared as a bride adorned for her husband."[26]

In Brief:

2028 "All Christians . . . are called to the fullness of Christian life and to the perfection of charity" (LG 40 # 2). "Christian perfection has but one limit, that of having none" (St. Gregory of Nyssa, De vita Mos.: PG 44, 300D).
2029 "If any man would come after me, let him deny himself and take up his cross and follow me" (⇒ Mt 16:24).

Council Vatican II, *Lumen Gentium*, Chapter V

The Universal Call to Holiness in The Church

39. The Church, whose mystery is being set forth by this Sacred Synod, is believed to be indefectibly holy. Indeed Christ, the Son of God, who with the Father and the Spirit is praised as "uniquely holy," loved the Church as His bride, delivering Himself up for her. He did this that He might sanctify her. (Cf Eph. 5:25-26) He united her to Himself as His own body and brought it to perfection by the gift of the Holy Spirit for God's glory. Therefore in

---

[23] Cf. 2 Tim 4.
[24] St. Gregory of Nyssa, Hom. in Cant. 8: PG 44, 941C.
[25] Cf. Council of Trent (1547): DS 1576.
[26] ⇒ Rev 21:2.

the Church, **everyone** whether belonging to the hierarchy, or being cared for by it, **is called to holiness**, according to the saying of the Apostle: "For this is the will of God, your sanctification". (1 Thess. 4.3; cf. Eph.1:4) However, this holiness of the Church is unceasingly manifested, and must be manifested, in the fruits of grace which the Spirit produces in the faithful; it is expressed in many ways in individuals, who in their walk of life, tend toward the perfection of charity, thus causing the edification of others; in a very special way this (holiness) appears in the practice of the counsels, customarily called "evangelical." This practice of the counsels, under the impulsion of the Holy Spirit, undertaken by many Christians, either privately or in a Church-approved condition or state of life, gives and must give in the world an outstanding witness and example of this same holiness.

40. The Lord Jesus, the divine Teacher and Model of all perfection, preached holiness of life to each and everyone of His disciples of every condition. He Himself stands as the author and consummator of this holiness of life: "Be you therefore perfect, even as your heavenly Father is perfect". (Mt. 5:48) Indeed He sent the Holy Spirit upon all men that He might move them inwardly to love God with their whole heart and their whole soul, with all their mind and all their strength (Cf. Mk. 12:30) and that they might love each other as Christ loves them. (Cf. Jn. 13.34; 15:12) The followers of Christ are called by God, not because of their works, but according to His own purpose and grace. They are justified in the Lord Jesus, because in the baptism of faith they truly become sons of God and sharers in the divine nature. In this way they are really made holy. Then too, by God's gift, they must hold on to and complete in their lives this holiness they have received. They are warned by the Apostle to live "as becomes saints", (Eph. 5:3) and to put on "as God's chosen ones, holy and beloved a heart of mercy, kindness, humility, meekness, patience", (Col. 3:12) and to possess the fruit of the Spirit in holiness. (Cf. Gal. 5:22; Rom. 6:22) Since truly we all offend in many things (Cf. Jas. 3:2) we all need God's mercies continually and we all must daily pray: "Forgive us our debts" (1 Mt. 6:12)

Thus, it is evident to everyone, that **all the faithful of Christ of whatever rank or status, are called to the fullness of the Christian life and to the perfection of charity**; by this holiness as such a more human manner of living is promoted in this earthly society. In order that the faithful may reach this perfection, they must use their strength accordingly as they have received it, as a gift from Christ. They must follow in His footsteps and conform themselves to His image seeking the will of the Father in all things. They must devote themselves with all their being to the glory of God and the service of their neighbour. In this way, the holiness of the People of God will grow into an abundant harvest of good, as is admirably shown by the life of so many saints in Church history.

41. **The classes and duties of life are many, but holiness is one** — that sanctity which is **cultivated by all** who are moved by the Spirit of God, and who obey the voice of the Father and worship God the Father in spirit and in truth. These people follow the poor Christ, the humble and cross-bearing Christ in order to be worthy of being sharers in His glory. Every person must walk unhesitatingly according to his own personal gifts and duties in the path of living faith, which arouses hope and works through charity.

In the first place, the shepherds of Christ's flock must holily and eagerly, humbly and courageously carry out their ministry, in imitation of the eternal high Priest, the Shepherd and Guardian of our souls. They ought to fulfil this duty in such a way that it will be the principal means also of their own sanctification. Those chosen for the fullness of the priesthood are granted the ability of exercising the perfect duty of pastoral charity by the grace of the sacrament of Orders. This perfect duty of pastoral charity is exercised in every form of episcopal care and service, prayer, sacrifice and preaching. By this same sacramental grace, they are given the courage necessary to lay down their lives for their sheep, and the ability of promoting greater holiness in the Church by their daily example, having become a pattern for their flock. (Cf. 1 Pt. 5:3)
Priests, who resemble bishops to a certain degree in their participation of the sacrament of Orders, form the spiritual crown of the bishops. They participate in the grace of their office and they should grow daily in their love of God and their neighbour by the exercise of their office through Christ, the eternal and unique Mediator. They should preserve the bond of priestly communion, and they should abound in every spiritual good and thus present to all men a living witness to God. All this they should do in emulation of those priests who often, down through the course of the centuries, left an outstanding example of the holiness of humble and hidden

service. Their praise lives on in the Church of God. By their very office of praying and offering sacrifice for their own people and the entire people of God, they should rise to greater holiness. Keeping in mind what they are doing and imitating what they are handling, these priests, in their apostolic labours, rather than being ensnared by perils and hardships, should rather rise to greater holiness through these perils and hardships. They should ever nourish and strengthen their action from an abundance of contemplation, doing all this for the comfort of the entire Church of God. All priests, and especially those who are called "diocesan priests," due to the special title of their ordination, should keep continually before their minds the fact that their faithful loyalty toward and their generous cooperation with their bishop is of the greatest value in their growth in holiness.

Ministers of lesser rank are also sharers in the mission and grace of the Supreme Priest. In the first place among these ministers are **deacons**, who, in as much as they are dispensers of Christ's mysteries and servants of the Church, should keep themselves free from every vice and stand before men as personifications of goodness and friends of God. (Cf. 1 Tim. 3:8-10 and 12-1) Clerics, who are called by the Lord and are set aside as His portion in order to prepare themselves for the various ministerial offices under the watchful eye of spiritual shepherds, are bound to bring their hearts and minds into accord with this special election (which is theirs). They will accomplish this by their constancy in prayer, by their burning love, and by their unremitting recollection of whatever is true, just and of good repute. They will accomplish all this for the glory and honour of God. Besides these already named, there are also **laymen, chosen of God and called by the bishop**. These laymen spend themselves completely in apostolic labours, working the Lord's field with much success.

Furthermore, **married couples** and Christian parents should follow their own proper path (to holiness) by faithful love. They should sustain one another in grace throughout the entire length of their lives. They should imbue their offspring, lovingly welcomed as God's gift, with Christian doctrine and the evangelical virtues. In this manner, they offer all men the example of unwearying and generous love; in this way they build up the brotherhood of charity; in so doing, they stand as the witnesses and cooperators in the fruitfulness of Holy Mother Church; by such lives, they are a sign and a participation in that very love, with which Christ loved His Bride and for which He delivered Himself up for her. A like example, but one given in a different way, is that offered by **widows and single people**, who are able to make great contributions toward holiness and apostolic endeavour in the Church. Finally, **those who engage in labour**—and frequently it is of a heavy nature—should better themselves by their human labours. They should be of aid to their fellow citizens. They should raise all of society, and even creation itself, to a better mode of existence. Indeed, they should imitate by their lively charity, in their joyous hope and by their voluntary sharing of each others' burdens, the very Christ who plied His hands with carpenter's tools and Who in union with His Father, is continually working for the salvation of all men. In this, then, their daily work they should climb to the heights of holiness and apostolic activity.

May all those who are weighed down with **poverty, infirmity and sickness**, as well as those who must bear various **hardships** or who suffer **persecution** for justice sake — may they all know they are united with the suffering Christ in a special way for the salvation of the world. The Lord called them blessed in His Gospel and they are those whom "the God of all graces, who has called us unto His eternal glory in Christ Jesus, will Himself, after we have suffered a little while, perfect, strengthen and establish". (1 Pt. 5:10)

Finally **all Christ's faithful, whatever be the conditions, duties and circumstances of their lives**—and indeed through all these, will daily increase in holiness, if they receive all things with faith from the hand of their heavenly Father and if they cooperate with the divine will. In this temporal service, they will manifest to all men the love with which God loved the world.

42. "God is love, and he who abides in love, abides in God and God in Him". (1 Jn. 4:16) But, God pours out his love into our hearts through the Holy Spirit, Who has been given to us;(Cf. Rom. 5:5) thus **the first and most necessary gift is love**, by which we love God above all things and our neighbour because of God. Indeed, in order that love, as good seed may grow and bring forth fruit in the soul, each one of the faithful must willingly hear the Word of God and accept His Will, and must complete what God has

begun by their own actions with the help of God's grace. These actions consist in the use of the sacraments and in a special way the Eucharist, frequent participation in the sacred action of the Liturgy, application of oneself to prayer, self-abnegation, lively fraternal service and the constant exercise of all the virtues. For **charity**, as the bond of perfection and the fullness of the law, (Cf. Col. 3:14; Rom. 13:10.) **rules over all the means of attaining holiness** and **gives life** to these same means. **It is charity which guides us to our final end. It is the love of God and the love of one's neighbour which points out the true disciple of Christ.**

Since Jesus, the Son of God, manifested His charity by laying down His life for us, so too no one has greater love than he who lays down his life for Christ and His brothers.(Cf. 1 Jn. 3:16; Jn. 15:13) From the earliest times, then, some Christians have been called upon—and some will always be called upon—to give the supreme testimony of this love to all men, but especially to persecutors. The Church, then, considers martyrdom as an exceptional gift and as the fullest proof of love. By martyrdom a disciple is transformed into an image of his Master by freely accepting death for the salvation of the world—as well as his conformity to Christ in the shedding of his blood. **Though few are presented such an opportunity, nevertheless all must be prepared to confess Christ before men. They must be prepared to make this profession of faith even in the midst of persecutions, which will never be lacking to the Church, in following the way of the cross.**

Likewise, the holiness of the Church is fostered in a special way by the observance of the counsels proposed in the Gospel by Our Lord to His disciples. An eminent position among these is held by virginity or the celibate state.(Cf 1 Cor. 7:32-34) This is a precious gift of divine grace given by the Father to certain souls,(Cf Mt. 19:11; 1 Cor.7:7) whereby they may devote themselves to God alone the more easily, due to an undivided heart. (14*) This perfect continency, out of desire for the kingdom of heaven, has always been held in particular honour in the Church. The reason for this was and is that perfect continency for the love of God is an incentive to charity, and is certainly a particular source of spiritual fecundity in the world.

149

The Church continually keeps before it the warning of the Apostle which moved the faithful to charity, exhorting them to experience personally what Christ Jesus had known within Himself. This was the same Christ Jesus, who "emptied Himself, taking the nature of a slave . . . becoming obedient to death", (Phil. 2:7-8) and because of us "being rich, he became poor". (2 Cor. 8:9) Because the disciples must always offer an imitation of and a testimony to the charity and humility of Christ, Mother Church rejoices at finding within her bosom men and women who very closely follow their Saviour who debased Himself to our comprehension. There are some who, in their freedom as sons of God, renounce their own wills and take upon themselves the state of poverty. Still further, some become subject of their own accord to another man, in the matter of perfection for love of God. This is beyond the measure of the commandments, but is done in order to become more fully like the obedient Christ.

Therefore, all the faithful of Christ are invited to strive for the holiness and perfection of their own proper state. Indeed they have an obligation to so strive. Let all then have care that they guide aright their own deepest sentiments of soul. Let neither the use of the things of this world nor attachment to riches, which is against the spirit of evangelical poverty, hinder them in their quest for perfect love. Let them heed the admonition of the Apostle to those who use this world; let them not come to terms with this world; for this world, as we see it, is passing away.(Cf 1. Cor. 7:31ff.)

Novo millennio ineunte (John Paul II)

Holiness

30. First of all, I have no hesitation in saying that **all pastoral initiatives must be set in relation to *holiness***. Was this not the ultimate meaning of the Jubilee indulgence, as a special grace offered by Christ so that the life of every baptized person could be purified and deeply renewed?

It is my hope that, among those who have taken part in the Jubilee, many will have benefited from this grace, in full awareness of its demands. Once the Jubilee is over, we resume our normal path, but knowing that stressing holiness remains more than ever an urgent pastoral task.

It is necessary therefore to rediscover the full practical significance of Chapter 5 of the Dogmatic Constitution on the Church *Lumen Gentium,* dedicated to the "universal call to holiness". The Council Fathers **laid such stress** on this point, not just to embellish ecclesiology with a kind of spiritual veneer, but to make **the call to holiness an intrinsic and essential aspect of their teaching on the Church**. The rediscovery of the Church as "mystery", or as a people "gathered together by the unity of the Father, the Son and the Holy Spirit", was bound to bring with it a rediscovery of the Church's "holiness", understood in the basic sense of belonging to him who is in essence the Holy One, the "thrice Holy" (cf. *Is* 6:3). To profess the Church as holy means to point to her as *the Bride of Christ,* for whom he gave himself precisely in order to make her holy (cf. *Eph* 5:25-26). This as it were objective gift of holiness is offered to all the baptized.

But **the gift in turn becomes a task, which must shape the whole of Christian life**: "This is the will of God, your sanctification" (*1 Th* 4:3). It is a duty which concerns not only certain Christians: "All the Christian faithful, of whatever state or rank, are called to the fullness of the Christian life and to the perfection of charity".

31. At first glance, it might seem almost impractical to recall **this elementary truth as the foundation of the pastoral planning** in which we are involved at the start of the new millennium. Can holiness ever be "planned"? What might the word "holiness" mean in the context of a pastoral plan?

In fact, **to place pastoral planning under the heading of holiness is a choice filled with consequences**. It implies the conviction that, since Baptism is a true entry into the holiness of God through incorporation into Christ and the indwelling of his Spirit, it would be a contradiction to settle for a life of mediocrity, marked by a minimalist ethic and a shallow religiosity. To ask catechumens: "Do you wish to receive Baptism?" means at the same time to ask them: "Do you wish to become holy?" It means to set before them **the radical nature of the Sermon on the Mount**: "Be perfect as your heavenly Father is perfect" (*Mt* 5:48).

As the Council itself explained, this ideal of perfection must not be misunderstood as if it involved some kind of extraordinary existence, possible only for a few "uncommon heroes" of holiness. The ways of holiness are many, according to the vocation of each individual. I thank the Lord that in these years he has enabled me to beatify and canonize a large number of Christians, and among them many lay people who attained holiness in the most ordinary circumstances of life. **The time has come to re-propose wholeheartedly to everyone this** *high standard* of *ordinary Christian living:* the whole life of the Christian community and of Christian families must lead in this direction. It is also clear however that the paths to holiness are personal and call for a genuine *"training in holiness"*, adapted to people's needs. This training must integrate the resources offered to everyone with both the traditional forms of individual and group assistance, as well as the more recent forms of support offered in associations and movements recognized by the Church.

The Epiphany of "The Church of The Desert"

The meaning of the Prophetic branch of the Church

What can a better knowledge of the structure of the Church offer to our Spiritual Life? The following text is on the "Prophetic Branch" of the Church. It is an important one. It is like an epiphany (the revelation) of a hidden albeit vital aspect of the Church. What appears to us in the Church does not encompass all that the Church is. There are hidden treasures in the Prophetic Branch of the Church, or the "Church of the Desert"; we need to discover them because they are relevant for each one of us.

Spiritual Ecclesiology
Spiritual Life and the Structure of the Church

The structure of the Church is not static or constituted of equal bodies with no interaction. On the contrary it is dynamic, and its bodies interact amongst each other. Essentially, the Church is constantly "under construction": remember St. Paul (1 Corinthians and others) as well as St. Peter mentioning the fact that the Church is a "construction" and that Christ is its Cornerstone. There is an inner tension or dynamism in the Church as it constantly constructs and reconstructs itself.

We can keep this image of construction or also add to it the image of biological growth: just think of the growth of a tree, or of a human being. The "construction" image has the advantage of helping us see that we need to aim at completing the entire building. Each one of the faithful is like one more added brick. The image of biological growth greatly enhances the fact of the growth of the Church as one. The Church is the Body of Jesus.

The Church is being driven by three forces contributing to its construction. Each is different but they work together. The Prophetic force (latin: *munus*), the Priestly one, and finally the Kingly one. Each force is represented by a body in the Church.

1- The Bishops and the Pope embody or incarnate the Kingly force. As successors of the Apostles, they are 'Masters of Perfection', they lead the two other bodies with discernment as well as governing them.

2- The second Body in the Church consists of the Parishes with their Priests and the Faithful. They embody the Priestly force for construction. This is the largest base on which the Bishops and the Pastoral Ministry of the Church focus their attention. Usually everyone who becomes a Christian does so in a Parish, and his or her initial Growth through the first initiation sacraments (Baptism, Confirmation, Eucharist) is nurtured here. Every person starts first by belonging to this Body, as is so beautifully expressed by St. Augustine who says to his Flock: 'I am faithful with you, and Priest for you'.

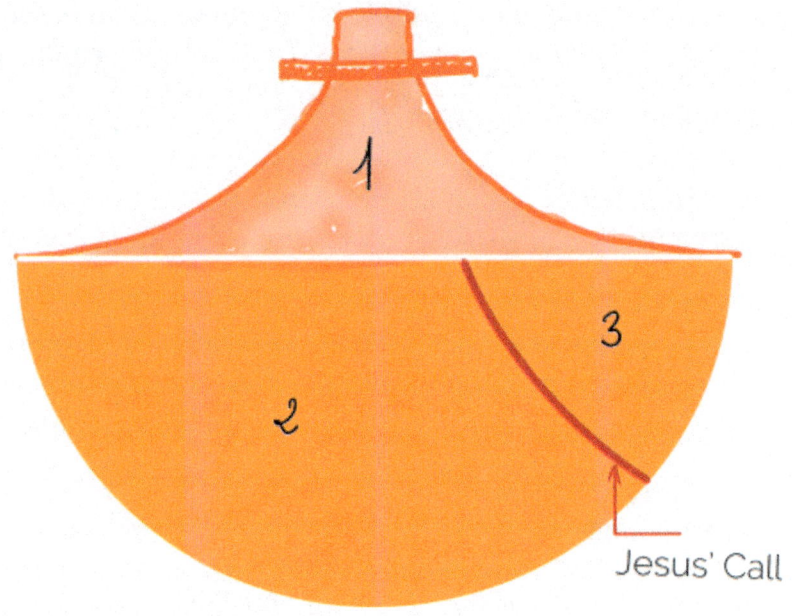

Jesus' Call

A

Possible modelling of the three Branches of the Church

3- Finally, the third Body in the Church is the Prophetic one. It consists of the 'Doctors and the Prophets' (see Acts 13:1): the theologians, the teachers and their institutes, universities, schools and the consecrated persons: monks, religious, secular institutes, new movements, virgins, missionaries…. They live holiness, they teach holiness, and they pray and worship, offering their entire life to God and to the Church. The core aspect of this body of the Church is a specific Call from Jesus to follow Him more closely ("come and follow me"). Becoming a Theologian is a real call and

154

one of the hardest. Amongst these "Doctors and Prophets" we have Masters of Spiritual Life (Master of Novices), Abbots, Spiritual Directors.

The main two bodies where growth occurs are the Priestly body and the Prophetic one. But they have different implications (size wise, tasks wise) and proceed at different speeds. The prophetic one is powerful, very focused and accelerated (with exponential growth) with the privilege of having tried and tested ways of life, a Body of Teaching and rules or ways of life that lead to holiness.

Again, the core interest in the "construction" of this "edifice" is the construction of the main body of the Church, the Priestly one. But the length, width, height and depth of that growth is simply holiness, and nothing less that it. Who is in charge of offering the teaching, discernment and experience in this field? It is the second Branch of the Church, the Prophetical one. Who is the yardstick in holiness? It is the Prophetical Branch.

The part that each of these branches takes in the construction process is different. One is the foundational phase and the other is the further "growth to the fullness" phase.

We can see this in the structure itself of the main document of the Council Vatican II on the Church: "Lumen Gentium". There is a total of eight chapters that describe the Church. Three of them are on each one of the bodies:

> Chapter III is on the Bishops
> Chapter IV is on Lay people
> Chapter VI is on the person who follows Jesus more closely.

But before going from Chapter IV to Chapter 6 we have Chapter V that is the starting point of this new dynamism, which is the deeper spiritual life or "consecrated life". Chapter V is the Call for Holiness. It is the hinge. This is the Call that will explain the new dynamism we find in Chapter VI and the benefits of crossing from IV to VI.

Understanding the deeper dynamic aspect of the structure of the Church is very important. All its life and activities tend toward holiness. There is therefore a healthy "tension" generated by the vital necessity for growth. He who does not doesn't go forward goes backward on the journey toward the fullness of holiness.

The Mansions of the Church

As we have said above, the Church is Jesus himself. Christ is our Way, the Journey toward the fullness of the Father. Therefore, the Church is "Christ our Way". She is all-together, the final place for all who are holy and united to Christ and with Him, and the journey itself that leads to the final place. The journey has different stages and dwelling places. In fact, the great doctors of the Church present us with the journey as divided into various steps, until we reach Union with Christ and finally reach the fullness of his height and love. This means that there are various dwelling places in the Church herself, each one hosting whoever has reached it and preparing its actual dwellers to cross to the following dwelling place. The journey we are talking about here is a journey of transformation, sanctification (divinisation).

The Church is the Lord Himself, His body. He receives us in his body, He and His Spirit are in charge of our sanctification. At each stage or set of stages the Church collaborates with the Lord and His Spirit in order to help in the work of Sanctification of the individuals. This has been the Lord's desire from day one when He chose and called various individuals to "be with Him", so they could learn from Him how to help others to grow. This experience has been transmitted from generation to generation till today.

The Two Branches of The Church

Each stage of growth needs a specific help. An allusion to this is given to us by St. Paul when he talked about "milk" and "solid food" (see I Corinthians 3:2; see also: Hebrews 5:12; 1 Peter 2:2).

The different sets of stages themselves are "managed" by different entities or branches in the Church.

The Church itself is divided into Dioceses. Each Diocese is managed by a Bishop (in bigger Dioceses the main Bishop is helped by other bishops). A mature Diocese would have developed the Prophetic Branch and therefore would contain all the stages.

The first branch is the "Priestly" Branch, or more plainly called: the Parishes. The second one is the Prophetic Branch. It includes: hermits, monks, religious, consecrated, new movements of the Church and all those who have heard the Call of Jesus and who follow Him more closely.

Each one of the two branches has various stages in it. Each branch is "managed" (the help given for growth) by its specific leaders. Thus, the

Parish Priests manage the Priestly Branch, while the Masters of Spiritual Life manage the Prophetic one.

The hinge between the two branches is what we usually name: "Jesus' Call" to follow Him more closely (please read the following articles on the Call). Some call it: the "second conversion". It is a personal call addressed by Jesus to a specific person at a specific moment in his or her life.

The Hinge Between the Two Branches

If we consider St. Teresa's book called "The Interior Castle", we find in it seven dwelling places, which are like seven different stages or levels of transformation. Amongst these one can distinguish two sets of dwelling places:

> the first three and
> the following four!

The hinge between them, is situated between the third and the fourth mansions: it is this Call made by Jesus in person to follow Him more closely. Here is how St. Teresa starts it:

*"Before I begin to speak of the fourth Mansions, it is most necessary that I should do what I have already done — namely, commend myself to the Holy Spirit, and beg Him from this point onward to speak for me, so that you may understand what I shall say about the Mansions still to be treated. For we now begin to **touch the supernatural** and this is most*

difficult to explain unless His Majesty takes it in hand, as He did when I described as much as I understood of the subject, about fourteen years ago. Although I think I have now a little more light upon these favours which the Lord grants to some souls, it is a different thing to know how to explain them. May His Majesty undertake this if there is any advantage to be gained from its being done, but not otherwise.

As these Mansions are now getting near to the place where the King dwells [the seventh Mansion], they are of great beauty and there are such exquisite things to be seen and appreciated in them that the understanding is incapable of describing them in any way accurately without being completely obscure to those devoid of experience. But any experienced person will understand quite well, especially if his experience has been considerable. It seems that, in order to reach these Mansions, one must have lived for a long time in the others; as a rule one must have been in those which we have just described, but there is no infallible rule about it, as you must often have heard, for the Lord gives when He wills and as He wills and to whom He wills, and, as the gifts are His own, this is doing no injustice to anyone." (St. Teresa of Avila, "The Interior Castle", Mansions 4:1)

We can say that the first three mansions are managed by the Parish Priest, and the normal place for them is the Parish. The four following mansions (from 4 to 7) are managed by the Spiritual Masters (the Leaders of consecrated life) and their different places are: the monastery, the convent, some new movements of the Church.

Both branches are under the supervision and vigilance of the Bishop and his collaborators. It is true that some religious orders are under the direct supervision of the Holy See, but any/all parts of their ministry in the Diocese remains under the supervision of the local Bishop

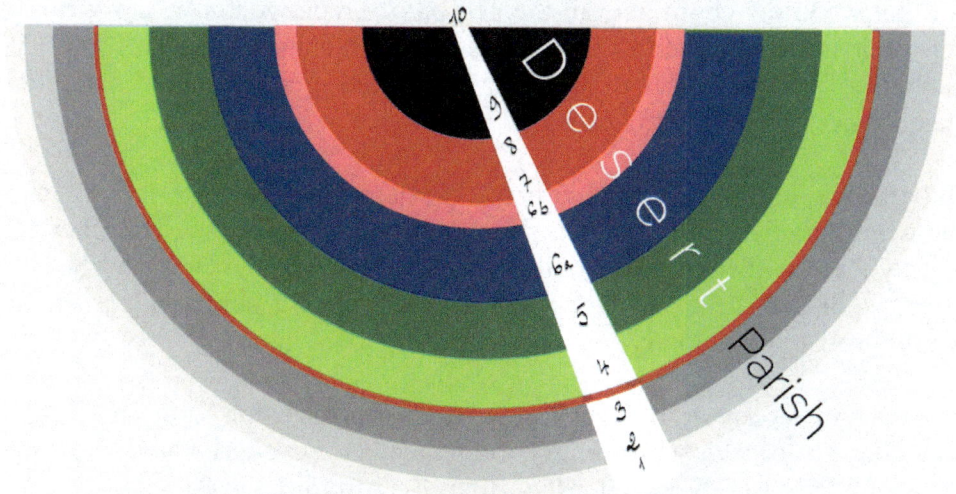

Spiritual Ecclesiology

Modelling of the two Branches from a spiritual point of view

The Second Conversion

St. Teresa's life itself is of great use to us because it helps us understand her teaching in the correct light, namely, she first experiences what she then describes in her teaching. We see, then, that she is first guided by the Holy Spirit through her Spiritual Masters, followed then by her experience of the Risen Lord, which thereafter she describes in her teaching.

Although Teresa of Avila enters into the Monastic life at nineteen years of age, her experience of Christ only undergoes a very radical change after roughly twenty years of religious life! And it is only then that her spiritual life takes off. Beforehand, she was oscillating between moments where she was doing well spiritually, and others (longer) where the opposite was true. In fact, the cause of this was the fact that her heart was divided between the Lord and some people of her acquaintance. Her heart was not given totally to the Lord. Therefore, she could not hear the Lord's Call clearly: as a consequence, she was not able to answer it and receive the abundance of Graces He wanted to give – as He wants to give each one of us.

All that we know about her, all the Teresa of Avila we know, her writings, her foundations, come after this conversion at the age of almost forty. This moment of conversion is the hinge we are talking about and characterises the entrance to the Fourth Mansions.

Only then would her heart be unified, her desire becoming to follow Jesus, she would give Him everything: she would allow Him to lead her, her way of praying would change, her daily life would change, the Grace of the Holy Spirit would start then to work wonders, showering her with graces. She would grow exponentially.

Let us now consider the life of another fundamental saint in order to understand more clearly the two branches of the church and the hinge between them. Let us consider the life of St. Anthony the Great.

St. Anthony The Great
Traditionally, St. Anthony the Great (third-fourth century A.D.) is considered to be the Father of all Monks (East and West). St. Benedict, by comparison, is the Father of all Western Monks only.

The life of St. Anthony, written by St. Athanasius, is an important foundational document. In a way it shows us the birth of Monastic life. It

160

shows us in a very clear "geographic" way the two branches of the Church. Initially St. Anthony, an orphan living with his sister, is living in a parish in lower Egypt. One day, while attending Mass, the Gospel that was proclaimed has included Jesus' Call to follow Him more closely: "go, sell what you have, give the money to the poor and come and follow me". Forthwith St. Anthony decided to seek out detachment in the desert, going into ever deeper isolation and living for years in a cave, in the quest for "nothingness" in order to find Jesus and be with him. When some brothers came to him after many years and asked him to be their Master, an historic moment in the life of the Church, as described by St. Athanasius, was reached. Although monastic life existed, although some communities already existed, what we are witnessing here is the official description of the birth of the Prophetic branch of the Church.

When St. Anthony was listening to the Gospel in his parish, he did not hear it in a normal way. He heard the words as being addressed to him personally by Christ. In fact, Christ used them to touch him, talk to his heart, and mostly, to call him to follow Him more intimately. Christ did not ask him to become a Parish Priest. This could have been the case! But his call is not to the Priesthood. This aspect, indeed, is not even mentioned by St. Athanasius in further stages of the story of St. Anthony. Why? Because this is not the core of the Call. The core of the call is to search for Jesus only. We can almost say that the core of the call is essentially Spiritual and characterised not by a priestly status, but by a lay status totally immersed in a spiritual Call for transformation.

Here we come face to face with the birth point of the Prophetic Branch, the Branch of the Church that is meant to harbour all those who are called to follow Jesus more closely. The "desert" is the geographical place of this Branch. And "desert" means absence of any distraction, of anything that can allure or attract and lead astray from the one thing: the Quest for Union with Christ. What characterises this Branch, right after Jesus' personal Call, is the total response of the person. This is why, there is a specific moment where one can hear the call, and not before (please read again the chapter: "A Call is a Call").

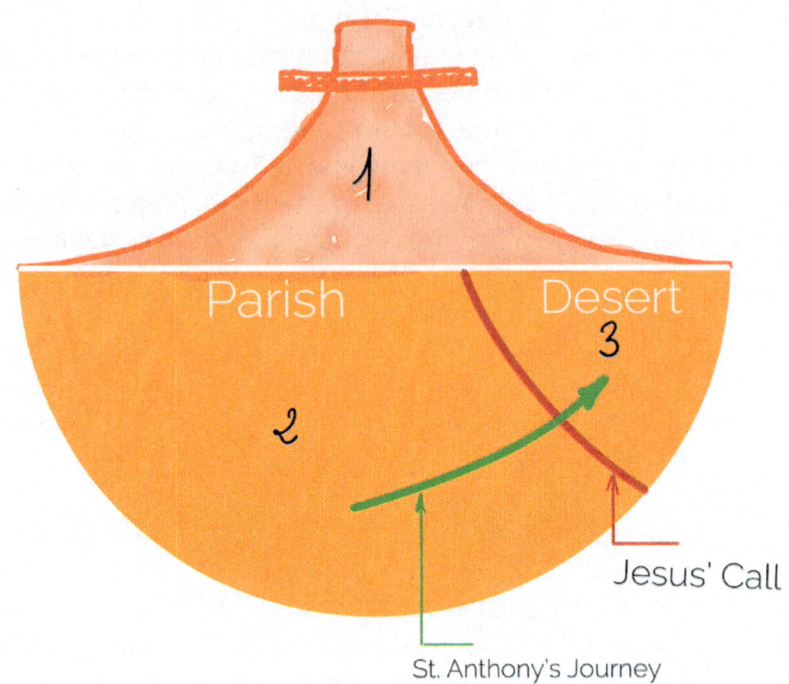

Parish

Desert

1

2

3

Jesus' Call

St. Anthony's Journey

As we can see, in the case of the Father of all Monks, the Father of the Prophetic Branch, the two branches are even geographically distinct: the Parish, in a city or town, and the Desert. The development of the different forms of following Christ more closely in the Prophetic branch will show us that it is not the physical geography that matters and characterises the "Desert" but that the "desert" is mainly an inner state. This is why many say today that our cities are like "deserts" where the quest for Union with Christ can be implemented. But we need to find the means that characterise the Prophetic Branch.

Drawing Spiritual Ecclesiology

Let us try to illustrate Spiritual Ecclesiology. In the drawing below, we have the different mansions represented in different colours. We include ten mansions and not seven as it exists in the case of St. Teresa of Avila, in order to show the continual growth in love until we reach its fullness in dying.

At this point it is worth reiterating that the first set of three mansions is the foundational work done in the parish by the Priestly Branch. The following mansions (4 to 9) are the ones that belong to the Prophetic Branch. As we can see, the Church's life is very dynamic, it all tends toward the union with Christ and the fullness of love. Growth or sanctification is its law.

Note: "6a" and **"6b"** is to differentiate between **"6a"** "the dark night of the spirit" (see St. John of the Cross') in St. Teresa's 6th mansions – hardly mentioned by her – and **"6b"** the "Spiritual Engagement" that follows it. **"8"** is meant to underline the growth in intensity of the love (Transformative Union, see St. John of the Cross "Living Flame of Love") with **"9"** being the participation in the Passion of the Lord. **"10"** is the Christian's sacred death, the final encounter with the Beloved as described by St. John of the Cross in the Living Flame of Love.

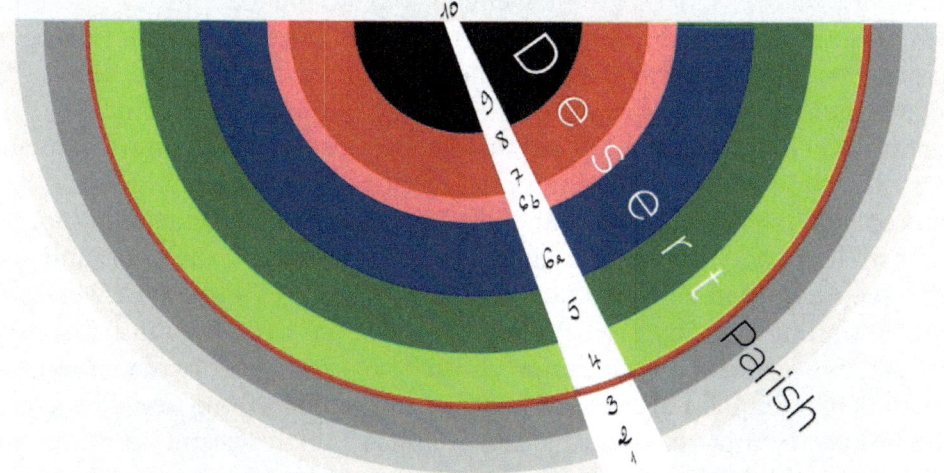

Spiritual Ecclesiology

The Epiphany of the Church of the Desert

The Church does not consist of one dwelling place: the Parish. The Church has different Mansions. St. Teresa describes seven of them as we have seen. The Parish is in charge of Evangelisation and Catechesis: the first three mansions. The Desert is in charge of helping those who hear the call to follow Jesus more closely. Added to this the Bishop supervises not only the Parishes, but also the "Desert" dimension in his Diocese. This is why St.

163

Thomas Aquinas calls the Bishop: Master of Perfection, Perfection being the modus operandi of the Desert. This is why it rapidly became the habit for certain Eastern Apostolic Churches to choose future bishops from the Monasteries.

The section of the Church that is the "Desert", indeed, is the most striking and most powerful light for the world. If on one hand the Parish has to lay the foundations of human life, led by the ten commandments and catechesis, the Desert on the other hand is the area that shows the higher perfection to which the Lord came to call us. If the first is for everybody, the second stage requires the accomplishment of the first. This is how the Lord operated with the rich young man! When he asked Him: "Good Teacher, what good thing shall I do that I may have eternal life?", Jesus did not start by offering the deepest aspect of his message. He went back to the foundations: "if you want to enter into life, keep the commandments". The Lord is not even hinting at the existence of other ways. This is the path, this is the order to follow! In order to build a very high tower one has to lay the foundations first.

It is only when the young man said that he had observed the commandments from his youth, that is, stating indirectly that he had solid foundations, that Jesus opened the perspective of another dimension, far more demanding: "If you want to be perfect, go, sell what you have and give to the poor, and you will have treasure in heaven; and come, follow Me." (Matthew 19:21)

Jesus is Calling… many are called as He says, but even though it is to the next stage of growth, where things will take off and grow exponentially, it is very demanding, totally demanding: the gift of everything and of oneself! It comes as no surprise, then, that the young rich man became sad: he went away sorrowful, for he had great possessions" the greatest possession being oneself. We know how it took St. Teresa of Avila almost twenty years to really "sell everything", to leave her heart free and entire for Jesus, and to really start to follow Him.

She will constantly teach this point of her conversion: we take a lot of time to give ourselves!

As we can see, the most beautiful part of the Church: the Desert, and the Spiritual Doctrine of Jesus is very demanding. Drawing closer to God is very demanding! God is a Jealous God, in the sense that He wants everything, not by half measures! The absolute! And the reward is absolute: Himself, given to us! Nothing on earth or in heaven can equal this reward, to experience the fullness of the intimacy of God. But the cost of it is very dear: all of our being! Remember the widow, who gave apparently very little, but in fact gave all that she had to live on, and in the eyes of God gave more than all the others! She gave herself, denied herself, and preferred Christ above anything else.

The beauty of Christ is tough! He does not surrender himself totally if we do not! He takes what we give Him says St. Teresa of Avila, but He will not give himself totally unless we do so. Love burns!

"Many are called" (Mt 22:14)! Actually, all of us are called to Christ's Beauty. But how many will experience it in its fullness? How many will know Jesus divinely? Spiritual Doctrine is harsh! It takes everything! This is why this branch of the Church is truly called: the Desert.

The Church of the Desert should shine in our heart and mind. It should be honoured as the Jewel in the Crown of the Church. It should be present constantly. Should help us to plumb the depths of the Gospel, the depths of Christ, the depths of the Gift of God (John 4:10). If we hear Jesus' Call to follow Him more intimately, "Spiritual Formation" should become, indeed must become, the core of our interest (see this article about Spiritual Formation).

Ecclesiology and Spirituality

The crossing from the Priestly Branch to the Prophetic Branch, from the Parish (the Parish Community) to the "Desert" is a passage from one economy to another. From one perception of the Providence of God to another one that is totally different.

One is really Christian when he or she belongs to a Parish. No doubt about it. But there are many ways of being Christian! There are many ways for the Holy Spirit to work in us (please see this article on The Five Modes of Activity of the Holy Spirit).

When we belong to a parish, our way of being Christian does not necessarily place God above everything in our life. We pursue other terrestrial (often legitimate) goals, we use a mix of human means and spiritual means with a human modality. Even if we consider God a Being, the Source of everything in our life, we are still the ones who are holding the reins of our life. We are still the ones who decide what to do, where to go.... Jesus is not being followed closely. He is not yet our real leader, minute by minute, who orientates us, opens the way in front of us and with whom we have a personal relationship. Therefore, it is only generically that we can say in this case that we are following Jesus.

The full richness of the Mass is found here and there. But the way of participating in it is very different if you are in the Parish or in the Desert. The Mass itself, as a ritual remains exactly the same! But the way to celebrate it, the way of entering spiritually into it is very different! It corresponds to the difference between the "general help of the grace of God" and the "particular help". Remember the prayer, "lift up your heart", in the Mass! The Desert is the place that teaches you how to do it and is expert in discerning the inner depths as well as being the place and the place par excellence that lives it and from it.

The Mass celebrated in the Desert, in the desert way, is a real Transfiguration: the eyes of the Apostles were opened, they could see the Lord transfigured and the Gospel (Jesus) in dialogue with Moses (the Torah) and Elijah (the Prophets), see Luke 24. Yet again, the Mass celebrated in the desert way embodies a real the experience of meeting the Risen Lord, just as what happened to the Disciples of Emmaus, or even better still what happened when the Lord appeared to the Apostles in St. John Chapter 20, through closed doors. The Desert is nothing less than the Upper Room.

Summing up we can say that according to these two branches we have two faces of Christianity. The Parish tends to present Christian life in a binary way: "1" I am in a state of Grace (I went to confession and received Communion and continue to do my best to be a good Catholic), or "0": God forbid, I have sinned, and therefore I need to go to confession. After the Call of Jesus, however, our spiritual life starts to really move and take off. We start to have a greater perception of the notion of growth, transformation, sanctification, Union with Jesus. We no longer function in the binary 1/0/1 way, but instead we start to perceive the existence of an exponential curve of growth. Of course, we continue to go to confession, but it is growth that is now at the heart of our daily challenges. Our vision of Christianity, changes! We understand that there is a Desert, i.e. only God matters, nothing should distract us on our journey as we follow Jesus ever more intimately, and we understand that the Desert has different depths as the story of St. Anthony the Great, mentioned above, indicates where step by step he divests himself of self to enter into greater depths in the Spiritual Journey towards Union with Jesus.

Note: "Parish" and "Desert" as used in this article are not strictly only geographical demarcations for the two branches of the Church – the "Priestly" and the "Prophetic"! One can perfectly have received the Lord's Call to follow Him more closely, and have already started to do so, having started to receive Spiritual Formation, having one's daily schedule changed, having a spiritual director, and yet still live within the perimeters of one's parish and go and attend the different services in the Parish and take part in some activities. But the individual knows at this juncture that he or she is receiving his or her formation from the "Prophetic Branch" with all its specificity and richness. Discernment is important in order to alleviate the burden of not knowing who does what in the two branches and not to search for elements of the Prophetic Branch present in the Parish.

Conclusion

Last but by no means least, it is most important to remember that the Prophetic Branch, the Church of the Desert, this hidden aspect of the Church, is totally placed under the leadership of Our Lady, it is her personal domain, her private garden! It is the "best part" (Luke 10:42), as the Lord puts it in the Gospel. It is the most sacred place, the true domain of the book of the "Song of Songs". "Therefore, look! I will now allure her. I will make her go out to the wilderness, and will speak to her heart." (Hosea 2:14)

Let us remember that the word "desert" as it is used here is mainly an image, the image of the attitude to have as one endeavours to journey in the Prophetic Branch: being focused on Jesus, not becoming distracted by anything else, maintaining silence in order to listen to Jesus, solitude, recollection, Jesus being the "only one thing [..] necessary" (Luke 10:42). Let us remember also that this "desert" is called upon to flourish: "The wilderness and the dry land shall be glad; and the desert shall rejoice, and blossom as the rose." (Isaiah 35:1).

This is the most beautiful part of the Church, but it is also the most hidden one to the common churchgoer! One enters into it only when called! It is a sacred and private domain! The true Jewel in the Crown of the Church and as such deserves deep honour.

One thinks he or she knows the Church! One thinks he or she knows Christ. Absolutely not! The Church has a sacred garden! We can call it "Desert", we can call it "blossoming garden", "garden" being the synonym for Eden or Paradise. It is the place of the intimate encounter with Christ the Groom. Finally, if we asked the question "What does the Desert Church bring us?" the simple answer would be reiterated by the greatest saints, to name but a few, with St. Benedict answering: "I do not prefer anything else above Jesus", St. Francis adding: "Jesus is my everything" and finally St. Therese of the Child Jesus answering with: "Jesus is my only Love" – "Love" being written with a capital letter – "Nothing exists in my life out of Jesus. It is a love story between him and me!"

Reading: Regarding the Functions of the Church: John Henry Newman, Preface of the Third Edition of his book "Via Media".

Question

Hi Jean,
It is new and unfamiliar to me hearing your teaching describing **such a clear demarcation between the "parish" and the "desert"** since in many eastern churches the monastic life forms the pattern that all Christians are called to follow towards divine union (through practice of the Jesus prayer and prayer of the heart, fasting, spiritual warfare against the spiritual powers that are set against man's union with Jesus).
So that was why I asked at the beginning of our conversation how the vision of the School of Mary relates to the formation that takes place in the parish or ministries like Ascension where we are dealing with many "unformed" people. It sounds like the School of Mary seeks to fill a need for a preservation of the rich teachings of the spiritual life and is a place where those with a deeper call to conversion may come to from the parishes.
But that raises more questions for me since one of the key elements of the desert monasticism was **community**. The sharing of the thoughts with the elders, eucharist together on Sundays, reading together the sayings of the fathers. Monasteries have (or had) this built in their communities but where are non-monastics to receive these things? So I would love to hear where those who are introduced to the spiritual way of the desert through the School of Mary are recommended to find the community and

168

sacramental/liturgical life that often acts as a beating heart of the monastic way. Do you attend Mass at a monastery? If so which one? Do you recommend your students go back and act as leaven in the parishes? Etc. Thank you for indulging my interest. And I know you are very busy so don't feel pressured to respond quickly to my musings.
Christ's Peace,
D

Answer

Thank you, D., for your question/s. In order to answer them, I feel I need to clarify something about the three "munera" (*munera* plural of *munus*) or functions of Christ. They can be seen as personal qualities in Christ and in each Christian regardless of his or her call in the Church. But the whole Church, as Jesus' Bride, as Jesus' People, has the three characteristics. Not only that, but one can easily notice that the three qualities or functions can also be used to describe a function inside of the Church. We need to keep this in mind. For instance, any baptised person is king, priest and prophet in Christ. A Bishop for instance is rather to be considered in the Kingly function of the Church because he is called to govern a Diocese. Is there a hierarchy among these qualities? John Henry Newman tended to think there was in his writings (please see the long Introduction to the second edition of the *Via Media* which is a masterpiece in ecclesiology). Another example of this is the teaching mission or function of the Church seen as the Prophetic side. We can then easily go on to say that the Sanctification office of the Church is the Priestly function.

The distinction between the two uses of the three qualities and functions in Christ needs to be kept in mind. If the use of the first one is easy (since we are all baptised, we have a share in the three functions or qualities of Christ), the second needs greater refining.

John Henry Newman says that the Prophetic function of the Church (the entire Church) lies in the Teaching mission of the Church, and not only does it come first but it shapes everything in the Church and keeps the Church rooted in the Truth. Yes, the Truth, Jesus, the Word of God, is what forms the Church, shapes it, enlightens it, etc. We have remained with this understanding of the Prophetic side/function of the Church: see Congar and Hervé Legrand OP). Thus, for Newman, Universities (which teach

Theology) are one of the principal components of the Prophetic side/function of the Church as a whole.

The actual ecclesiology continues (essentially because of Newman and Congar's influence I think, and the feeling that what they say is obvious) to work and see things this way (See Vatican II theology and the following ecclesiological developments, theology and ordinary magisterium). One still feels it is a bit incomplete. I understand that it can be in a way confirmed by the history of the Church, the history of 18/19 centuries (and Newman takes various examples from the history of the Church), but still it fails to cover the entire reality of the Church. It is a good start to identify the three functions of Christ as different areas in the Church but how it is applied by Newman, I think, needs some refining.

How can this theological fine-tuning occur? The state of Spiritual Theology's since the 1940s in my humble view is very weak – many will not agree, but this is the reality. On the contrary, the change in methods that occurred in 1950s-1960s did not really improve the situation of Spiritual Theology. And we are still suffering because of this. In fact, since the methods in theology are today universal in the Catholic Church, we cannot see Spiritual Theology under a different light. But still, if Spiritual Theology were to be renewed – which I hope for – the Church's "structuring" according to the three *munera* will be able to be fine-tuned. Why? Because one of the main benefits of *Spiritual Theology* is to study in the greatest depth the work of the Holy Spirit in us. It allows us to see that He pursues a long journey of purification, transformation, divinisation. The more we study this journey, its characteristics, which proceed totally from the different forms of the work of the Holy Spirit in the human being, (according to the needs of each stage), the more a completely new light emerges. A greater understanding begins of a fundamental notion in Spiritual Theology, which, in fact, is mentioned in *Lumen Gentium* – the Call of Jesus. We start to see it as a real and radical turning point in the way the Holy Spirit works (in fact starts to work) in us. We start to understand more fully the distinction between "Catechesis" (see the Catechesis of the Fathers) and "Mystagogy" (see the Fathers of the Church mystagogies) and further stages mentioned by the Spiritual Masters (Origen, Dionisius, Gregory of Nyssa...). Till today, we know about their existence, but we do not really understand the real differences between them.

Note: Catechesis and Mystagogies were often given by Bishops and the Bishop normally covers and is responsible for the two areas: Parish and Desert. Furthermore, Bishops were not recruited from among monks in the East from the beginning, but only as of the fourth and fifth centuries.

In the Gospel, the Lord himself, states the existence of two phases where God is present, where we have duties (commandments) to fulfil toward Him: one before meeting Christ and one after meeting Him. See the Rich Young Man. Of course, then we had only Judaism, and now we have only Christianity so to speak. But within Christianity I can be "judaising" so to speak or "christianising", i.e. either I can be a Christian fulfilling the commandments ("have you observed the commandments and put them into practice?", Christ's first question to the young man), or I can be a Christian who becomes able to hear Jesus' Call and, by the Grace of God, has started to follow Him. The difference is huge between these two categories of Christians grace wise. Indeed, exteriorly both are baptised Christians. However, the Theology of religious life in Vatican II says that religious/monastic life is not a new category of Christians but a new depth in Baptism, like a greater new development of the seed of Baptism. But have we properly explored the awakening of this new stage of deepening?

You find this distinction in St. Antony the Great's Life, written by Athanasius the Great. Initially Antony was a committed Christian in his parish and it is in his parish attending the liturgy where he heard Jesus' call to a new life, where he is "in movement", starting to follow the Lord. You find this distinction throughout the history of the Church, everywhere. We call this phenomenon in the Western tradition "second conversion", or vocation.

From the first stages of the parish we move to another stage where the pastoral care is absolutely different, the spiritual teaching is different. The Mass and Liturgy of the Hours are the same, but the levels of depth and personal relationship with Jesus are completely different. Let us keep this in mind: the pastoral work is different and the doctrine also!

In St. Teresa of Avila's masterpiece, *The Interior Castle*, the turning point mentioned above occurs between the Third and Fourth Mansions. This means that one has a life as a Christian from outside the castle (Mansions 0) till Mansions Three included. Then you have a new life, from the Fourth onward till the Seventh. When we study her life and study her conversion, at almost forty years of age we find that it illustrates this change, the "starting of supernatural things" as she says. Not only the history of her conversion is fundamental, but it cannot really be understood without a thorough analysis of "Way of Perfection" where she points out the real problem: the need to have in the first phase a true total commitment (which in her case was lacking for about twenty years, as a nun!!), a thorough and perfect spiritual practice of the evangelical virtues.

So, bottom line: we have not two types of Christians but two stages of Growth: one from 0 to 3 and one from 4 to 7. You need people to attend to the needs of the work of sanctification in these two phases. Even if the Holy Spirit within each of these two phases works in different ways, we can easily distinguish the two groups in two phases. When St. Teresa of Avila starts the second phase she says: here start the "supernatural things "(see beginning of the Fourth Mansions). In this sense *The Interior Castle* is a book on Ecclesiology and maps it (see the diagram above).

Vatican II underlined with great force the "Call to Holiness" for all baptised, regardless of their state of life (see here). Admittedly, here the Council did something amazing which is to break the mould of the "state of life" as a condition of following Jesus closely. But there are plenty of other things the Council could not do and are left to further development and growth in history. For instance, one of them is the following: yes everybody is called to follow Jesus and seek holiness, but this is the theory: in practice does every person hear the Call? Receive the Call? (see these two articles: hereand there) It is one thing to theologically contemplate Baptism and say: because of baptism all are called to holiness. But despite the fact that this is a theological truth, on the ground, in real life, there is a period of structuring that has to come first (Mansions 0 to 3, or Catechesis and Adult Formation, serious Christian commitment in a parish) in order for us to become able to hear the Call. Becoming ready to hear the Call is another question entirely (see here). Sadly, we take this issue (hearing the Call) for granted, as being automatic, and this comes from a total lack of understanding of the notion of Growth and its Stages. This is why *Spiritual Theology*, when developed properly, will revolutionise Ecclesiology and Pastoral Ministry.

If we keep in mind the two big chunks (0-3 and 4-7), each great section of growth needs a specific pastoral work and a "place" for it to live in (as you are alluding to in your question).

Contemplating St. Anthony the Great's life, I find these two great sections of our Christian life illustrated in the simple geographical distinctions: on the one hand in city/town/village and on the other the journey in the desert towards the cave and then to the community he helps. Of course, as you noticed, the development throughout twenty centuries of the history of the growth of the Church is no longer confining the following of Jesus in the consecrated life, or even as a lay person, to a geographical area. Our big cities are today authentic deserts. Not only that, but during the life of St. Antony we have from the sayings of the Desert Fathers, these first great spiritual masters (the Elders), the story of the Alexandrian shoemaker who was greater in his spiritual efforts than Antony. Moved by God to go and visit him in Alexandria, St. Anthony learned from him a great lesson to continue his growth. Indeed, throughout Church history, East and West, we have lay people closely following Jesus.

In my humble view, for now, in order to clarify this aspect of the structure of the Church, I prefer to use the terms: "Parish" and "Desert" and I prefer to apply the "Prophetic" munus (function) of the Church to the "desert" and not to "universities" as St. John Henry Newman did (let us remember that both desert and parish have each its own theology to develop and benefit from (see here)). If somebody finds better wording or clarity, I am happy to consider it.

Note: I prefer really and completely not to distinguish excessively between the Western side of the Church and the Eastern one (be it Orthodox or Catholic) and this for many reasons. One of them is that the Eastern Churches did not undergo the huge challenges of the Western side of the

Church, so it is an unfair and unbalanced comparison even if the Eastern Churches are very much present in the West today. As a Catholic, I consider that everything we find in the West and everything in the East is one, despite the apparent differences and as a Catholic I need to learn from 2000 years of Church life experienced here and there. They are the two lungs Pope John Paul II reminded us to learn to breath with.

Now, coming to your question: Where can one find a place to attend a more spiritual life (liturgy, community, friendship etc)?
Well in recent years the Western Catholic Church has witnessed an amazing development of new movements in the Church, without forgetting also the birth and development of the Charismatic Renewal movement.

Despite this, I would like to lay great stress on two things interconnected: a community (a Parish or a Spiritual one) needs at least two things for it to function properly: 1- a true leader who knows his or her Spiritual Theology and 2- a Renewed True Spiritual Living Tradition and Doctrine.

I would not at all take for granted that the Eastern Church's spirituality right now is the living embodiment of these two elements in a renewed way capable of talking to today's faithful. The same applies for the West. I am aware that western and eastern leaders will beg to differ with my diagnosis but this cannot change the reality as I see it and the way I see it.

In the West we have new movements and plenty of ancient secular orders, but neither of the two needs mentioned above (1- Formed Leaders and 2- Renewed Spiritual Doctrine) are available. The East has the ancient doctrine very present, some modern authors quoting it, some monks giving talks on it and the Bishops being recruited from among the Monks. They might seem to be trying more and adhere more to the ancient Masters but is this enough? Well, one needs to be in the East to judge – I do not find it enough when faced with the pressures and needs of post-modern life.

The lack of clarity coming from a non-renewed *Spiritual Theology* will continue to keep all of us, East and West, floating in a big "minestrone", with a lack of proper Spiritual Masters and a lack of proper Renewed Spiritual Doctrine.

In the West and in the East we tend to copy-paste some ancient masters. Is this enough to take responsibly the duty and function of the Prophetical *Munus* of Christ? Oh, no! The Holy Spirit will not work without us. Why? Because this is God's will. He does not want to save us alone, without a total commitment of the Church. We are left, consequently, with the necessity to commit and work and serve. Humbly of course! Humbly.

So, bottom line: our lack today is not of Spiritual Communities: see how many secular orders we have, see how many movements we have in the Church, even new orders. What is lacking is Spiritual Masters formed and ready to serve and a Renewed Spiritual Doctrine, complete, practical, clear. Since we already have the Communities, the School of Mary tries, humbly to provide the other two elements which are badly needed.

The day we are able to say that theologically the Prophetic side of the Church is Mansions 4-7 and not Universities and Theology, the Church will rise and answer in a much better way/more completely the Call of Jesus.

Let us pray and work tirelessly for this.

I hope this helps

Printed in Great Britain
by Amazon